Voice of the Children

on how to improve the world

Edited by Ri Ferrier

LEAF AND STAR PUBLISHING

Published by Leaf and Star
1 Yew Tree Cottages, Cherington, Tetbury GL8 8SJ

Copyright © Ri Ferrier 2008

First published in Great Britain in 2008 by Leaf and Star

ISBN 978-0-9557567-1-9

www.leafandstar.co.uk

Front cover picture drawn by James Savage,
St Aidans Catholic Primary School, Merseyside

Back cover pictures drawn by children from
Rodborough Primary School, Stroud

Graphic design by Qwertyop
www.qwertyop.co.uk

This book is dedicated to the children

Thanks

I have had much support for Voice of the Children and would like to thank all those who have stood by me through this project. I would especially like to thank Arwyn DreamWalker, Judy Rose and my beloved Gig Binder for their unending support. I would like to thank my two beautiful children, Jed and Alden, who are a constant beacon of hope and inspiration. I would like to thank Rod and Hannah Shaw at Qwertyop for their patience and help. Thanks also go to Mr Oliver Goldfinch (Sir) who inspired me as a child and is still keeping me in check!

And finally, I would like to thank all those who have donated to this project:

Morning Star Lodge – German Lodge
Rainbow Fund
Andy Andrews
Katherine Attwater
Chanan Bonser
Michael Bonser
Graham Clarke
Lyn Clarke
Rachel Haines
Paul Hougham
John Horan
Sue Humphries
Nina Pennell
Kate Raggett
Mairead Tindall
Jean White

Foreword

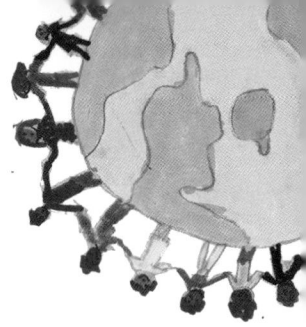

This book has been entirely written by children aged 9- 11. As a foreword, here are some of the things they are bringing to our attention:

"If I could change the world I would straight away,"
Jenna, Glasgow

"I would love wars in my world to stop."
Richard, Neath

"Give racism the red card."
James, Merseyside

"I want a world in which children can be free to go round the block by themselves."
Rebecca, Edinburgh

"We don't value life enough."
Joe, Stroud.

"People don't care, they aren't aware that the world that we live in soon wont be there."
Dylan, Glasgow

"All around the world, children dying, parents crying, Governments lying, what have we got to do?"
Victoria, Berkshire

"Across all continents we must come together, to make our world a better place forever."
Stephanie, Middlesex

"Global warming is my biggest fear – when I heard about it I shed a tear."
Megan, Somerset

"Why destroy when you can find and make? Let's re-cycle, lets re-create."
*From the Song **A Better World** on the enclosed CD by children at Dowson Primary School in Cheshire.*

Introduction

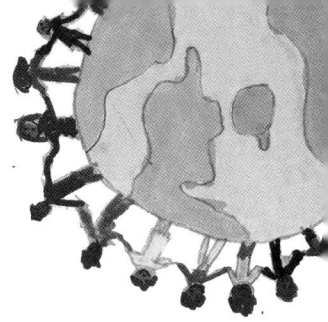

The idea for **Voice of the Children** came to me in a very strong dream; on waking the next day I knew that this was a project I had to manifest. In the dream, it was imperative that the children - the future guardians of the earth - had an input on the world they would be inheriting. There needed to be a bridge built between the children and the decision-makers - specifically Members of Parliament.

Voice of the Children has been sent, with my compliments, to *every* MP in the UK. Even if just one MP takes the time to listen to what the children are calling for, then this project has been worthwhile.

There are many poems, plays, drawings, raps and songs in this book. Children, aged 9-11, all answered the question: "How would you improve the world?" I placed no creative restriction on their work: no specific format, no specific topic. The children's work appears as it was presented to me – I have not corrected their spelling or grammatical errors.

Their responses have far exceeded my expectations. I have been inspired and moved to hear what they have to say. I know you too will feel the same. Their response is unselfish, untainted by those dream-killers of 'I can't' or by the corruption of power. Their message is pure and simple in its essence - yet covers the topics on most political agendas: global warming, poverty, education, war, child-abuse and bullying.

It is our responsibility as adults to hear these children, to take action to provide them with the world they deserve. It is every child's right to have a home, security, love, food and water. In this day and age, it is disgusting that this is not so. It is even more disgusting that we as a race are irreparably harming even more of the legacy that we leave to the children.

It is easy to become overwhelmed and not to act at all. It is easy to forget that even individuals can make a difference. For the children's sake, do NOT forget.

Voice of the Children calls you to act, to stand for the children, to stand as guardians for their future. If you feel moved to comment, please leave messages via my website: www.leafandstar.co.uk.

With blessings

Ri Ferrier
Leaf and Star

The World is drowning….

Hurricanes fly through the air
Waters flooding everywhere
Life will surely come to an end
Unless human nature turns a bend

Now the hot weather is beginning
Even the birds have ceased their singing
Since the dreadful droughts have started
Mother Nature has departed.

Tsunamis are soon on their way
Coming closer by the day
Homes will be obliterated
Leaving people devastated

The ice caps have begun to melt
The impact of this will be felt
As the world is rapidly warming
Intruding insects start swarming

Hurricanes flew through the air
Waters flooded everywhere
Now the devastation has vanquished
Mankind has been left to languish.

"I wrote this poem because I hope that
the dreadful events of the summer
floods will make everyone sit up and
take global warning seriously".

Harvey Brook, aged 11,
Rodborough Primary School, Stroud

Connor You'll Change Some Day
(to the tune of we will we will rock you)

Connor you're a kid make a big noise
Hanging in the street gonna be a big man
Some day
You got drugs in your face
You big disgrace
Kickin' your friends all over the place

We will we will change you
We will we will change you

Connor you're a young man hard man
Shoutin' in the street gonna destroy
Yourself some day
You got blood on yo' face
You big disgrace
Smashing and bashing all over the place

We will we will change you
We will we will change you

Connor you're a mess and in a jam
Begging on your knees gonna stop some
day

You got shame on you face
You big disgrace

Somebody better put you back in your
place

We will we will change you
We will we will change you

Beatrice Taylor, aged 9,
Budbrooke Primary School, Warwick

If I could change the world

If I could change the world I would straight away. The world would be much cleaner,
safer and be a pleasant place. The world is like a big rubbish dump full of problems
and mess. It would be much better if we helped our giant world because its such a
mess. We should stop smoking, child abuse and lots of different things. People under 21
should not be allowed to buy fireworks, unless you have I.D. Fireworks are giant colourful explosions that can be dangerous and dreadful in different ways. So lets help our
world out, come on its so easy!

Jenna Massey, aged 10,
Thornwood Primary School, Glasgow

The Magic Box

I will put in the box
the first flap of a dove,
the juiciest olive of the highest olive tree,
the brightest colour in the rainbow.

I will put in the box
the first smile of a snowman,
the last bark of a dog,
the heaviest tear drop in the world.

I will put in the box
the loudest shout of my ancient Grandad,
hearing the biggest bang in World War Two,
the waves from the oceans barrier.

I will put in the box
the brightest star in the sky,
the coolest wind,
the burnt sun in the sinking sand.

My box is fashioned from Greek Gold,
with peace in the corners and silence on the lid,
its hinges are steel from old cars.

I shall skate on my box
through the golden sand,
then sail away through the oceans grief
that never ends.

By **Jordan Swindells**, aged 10, Moorfield Primary School, Cheshire

How to make the world a better place

Less plastic, less waste
Then it would be a better place
Lose your car and walk instead
Or maybe we will all be dead
More plants, more grass
Get rid of all the gas
We're losing the world quite fast
So we might be the last

Philippa Bricklebank, year 6,
Braunston CE Primary School, Daventry

Save the Planet

Don't get a car - get a bike
And if you're a toddler get a trike
Walk to work, walk to school
And if you don't then you're not cool
You'll get fit if you walk more
and ride a bike if your feet get sore
Don't be lazy, don't slack
Get outside, get off your back.

We should try to improve the world
and make it a better place!

Charlotte Lyon, year 6,
Braunston CE Primary School, Daventry

Keep the world so tidy

If you keep the world so tidy
If you keep the world so clean
If you keep the world so tidy
You will get the beat

If you pick up all your rubbish
If you recycle all your paper
If you don't use as much card
You will get the beat

You could save the world by cleaning
You could save the world by recycling
You could save the world by litter picking
Everywhere you go

Aaron Hart,
Braunston CE Primary School, Daventry

A CLEAN, GREEN WORLD

Stop dropping litter

And tidy the place

Recycle every day

And try to replace.

Say no to pollution

That dirties the air

That's a good solution

Help the world to share.

Callum Foster, aged 9,
Canmore Primary School, Dunfermline

There are lots of ways of making the planet better. The main ones are electricity, oil and animals. There are ways of saving all of these by doing easy things like turning off lights when you go out the room or cutting down on foods like cod and haddock.

Electricity is one of the main problems because it is polluting but we need it. If everyone cut down then it will last longer. Also by using electricity you are polluting which is adding to the hole in the ozone layer. When the ozone layer is gone the climate will increase massively and that will make the Poles hotter and eventually melt them. When you recycle you are saving a lot of energy. Just one can can run a television for over four hours. Recycling is easy. You can recycle anything paper, cardboard, glass of a lot of metal. Plastic is sometimes harder. Plastic bags actually kill animals like seals, birds or even penguins! Some supermarkets recycle plastic but not many.

Another problem is endangered animals. Most people don't know but cod and haddock are nearly extinct. Pigs and chickens are much more common but many animals will not be allowed to be sold as food in the future. If you eat a mix of animals and pasta or rice it is a lot more healthy and it is good for the animals.

Alex Doran, aged 10, The Grange Junior School, Cheshire

Dear Prime Minister,

I would like to propose the following, which in my opinion, would make the world a better place:

Stop illegal hunting.
Government should give more money to help the poor.
Stop cutting down trees in forests because of global warming and it spoils animal habitats.

I think you should have much stronger punishments for people who kill animals for money. We as a nation should ensure that the animals are protected.

We should make sure that poverty doesn't exist anywhere in the world.

Yours sincerely
Charlie Ackland
Collis Primary School
Middlesex

Save our Universe!

Pollution, pollution, pollution,
There seems to be no solution.
There's rubbish and litter everywhere,
It seems that people don't really care.
The Universe is breaking apart,
They think its just a great big piece of art.
Pulling and straining, to never stop,
People will do that until they drop.
The rivers are overflowing,
Without any people knowing.
We are treating our world with no care
We keep doing it like it's a paper to tear.
Let's try to make our world a better place,
Please do NOT make it a DISGRACE!!

Cristina O'Brien, aged 10,
St Cecilia's Catholic Primary School, Surrey

Making Britain Green

If you make Britain clean
You will make people happy
Use diesel for your car
Get more bin men
Recycle more stuff
Like newspaper
Only use guns for the army and police
Don't spraypaint
Sell less drugs
People use drugs to act big
Everybody will be happy
People might get scared
They swear all the time
People might think their child
Might copy
Them
Don't break windows
More bottles

Sean Todd, aged 9,
Thornwood Primary School, Glasgow

GOODRICH CE (VC) PRIMARY SCHOOL
Head Teacher A.F.P.Griffiths

Goodrich CE (VC) Primary School
Goodrich
Ross on Wye
Herefordshire

Phone: 01600 890422
Fax: 01600 890827
Email: admin@goodrich.herefordshire.sch.uk
www.goodrichprimary.ik.org

Good manners do not cost anything, but are worth a lot
School Motto

Dear Mr.Brown,

I think, we as one world, should help to protect our environment and surroundings around us by recycling more.

We would also like it if we could donate more money to medicines and research for global warming.

We could also give money to all schools around the globe; to raise this money we could hold more fund-raising events for children and also more contests.

We should advertise more on the television about global warming and how we can stop it!

I believe we can do this if we really try hard and you as a parliament can help us to build a better world.

Yours Faithfully,

Rhys
Owen
And
Jack
Whittaker.

HEREFORDSHIRE EDUCATION DEPARTMENT

Rhys Owen, Jack Whittaker
Goodrich CE (VC) Primary School Ross on Wye

Improve the world

Stop vandalism or you will go to prison,
Don't cut down trees, save the bees,
Stop thugs from taking drugs,
Stop crime, it's wasting time,
Save nature, it's in danger
This is how you can improve the world.

Rebecca High, aged 9,
St John's Primary School, Barrhead

World Peace

You can give up your house
You can give up your books
You can give up your maids
and your cooks and your looks
But you can bring them all back
with some money and wealth
But you can't bring back a life
with its time and its health

Eleanor Overton, aged 10, Lavant
House School, Chichester

Dustmen, Dustmen- *an action rhyme*

Dustmen, dustmen go away,
Come back another day.
We have nothing in our bin,
We've been recycling!

Paper, bottles, cardboard, glass,
Drink cans, food tins, junk mail,
So.... pass....
By us

Dustmen, dustmen go away,
Come back another day.
We have nothing in our bin,

We've been recycling!

By the boys of Year 5 and Year 6
Hurworth House School, Darlington

**It's fun making up your recycling list-
It's even more fun saving all of it!**

If I Could Change the World

I would love wars in my world to
stop. If war keeps on it will
destroy my world and yours. I
want polluting in my world and
yours to stop before its too late
and flooding causes global
warming. I want to see an end
to bullying forever. Big children
should stop being nasty and start
being nice. I'm nice but I don't
want everyone to be just like me I
want them to be
themselves. And thank you for
listening to me.

Richard Lewis, aged 10, Clun Primary
School, Neath

Help Save The World

I would improve the world by sending clothes, and food to poorer countries because
they don't have as much as us. We could ask the rulers of the world to meet and try to
stop racism, bombing and wars. We could send doctors all around the world to help
cure diseases. Why don't we have more recycling bins and boxes? Why don't we use
less cars, and more buses could save our air.

Meghna Rao, aged 10, Lavant House School, Chichester

I would like more

 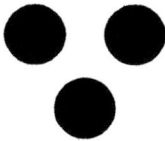 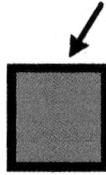

sun because it would

make people happy .

Nathan J

Nathan Johnston aged 10
Fleming Fulton School Belfast

A Better World

The world is precious place
So treat it well

So come on, people are starving
There aren't alway good drugs
theres sometimes bad ones
Why Why Why don't we think of
what we're doing?

Lets improve by not dropping litter
Stop rasism and deforesation.
There should be more recycling
Lets make peace not war

Think of people outside our lives
Think of animals letstry and save them
So come and stop the pollution more making.
and think more of our world

It is ill very very ill.
So why don't we make it better
Lets help the starving and
homeless.
Why don't we stop and give
them something.

There's people in Africa that don't have
anything lets give them something more than this.
lets give the world something more than this.

By Ellie and Hannah

Ellie and Hannah
St George's School for Girls Edinburgh

16

MY WORLD

Use both sides of a piece of paper so we don't have to cut down so many trees.

Insted of throwing things away after you've used them recycle them.

Turn off electricty when you go out of a room so you don't wase money.

Dont drive to places walk or cycle so you don't pollute the air

By Katy Frith 6L Age 10 The Grange

Katy Frith 6L
The Grange Junior School Cheshire

17

I would like everyone to live in a lovely castle

Alina

Alina
Limegrove School Limavady

MY WORLD :

NOW

Litter!

lots of electricity used even when it is not needed!

endangered animals!

Petrol running out!

Lots of trees chopped down!

Not very many clean hospitals!

the streets are homeless!

Polluted air!

WHEN I'M PRIMEMINISTER

Homes for the homeless

Water powered cars!

No Litter!

Cleaner hospitals!

Save animals

Only a few trees chopped down!

No smoking at all!!!

Some more clean air!

and lots more smiley faces

Olivia Exan-Treckett aged 10
The Grange Junior School Cheshire

19

If we could donate more money to the cause it would help People to recycle more.

We should also donate more money to cars so there would be less Global warming.

GLOBAL WARMING

If we could money donate to the council to convince Herefordshire to recycle more to save the planet.

Recycle!

Rhys Owen, Jack Whittaker
Goodrich CE (VC) Primary School Ross on Wye

20

Under Water Animals

endangered shark

me checking on the shark

Today there are thousand of endangered animals e.g the tiger shark is killed for it's fins so people can have soup. the are wiping out tuna clans every day.

Killing animals for there fur is wrong. Monkey. lepards, tigers and lion and many more.

On Land Animals In The Jungle

George Brooker aged 9
Longwick C of E Combined School Bucks

21

Reduce your carbon footprint
and world will be a better place
for me and you.

STOP NOW!!!!

Ban Smoking in England and Europe.
Stop Smoking it can clog up your arteries
and kill you.

HB

HB
stop

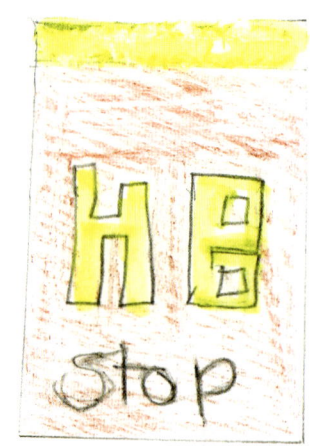

Georgia Needham, Ella Hutton, Peyton Sims aged 10
Longwick C of E Combined School Bucks

22

My perfect world

I'd love to live in a world
Where everyone is free,
A world that is happy and
healthy for everyone to see,
Where poverty and hunger is
lost without a trace,
Where we can live in harmony,
all religions, colours and race.
I wish nobody was rich and
then nobody would be poor,
Where nobody was greedy and
no one wanted more,
Where people were not selfish
and everyone would share.
A world thats full of kindness
and everyone will care.
By Nicola Kennedy age 9

Nicola Kennedy aged 9
St Margaret of Scotland Catholic Junior School Luton

BE SMART

LOOK AFTER THE WORLD

BE SMART, BE ECO FRIENDLY

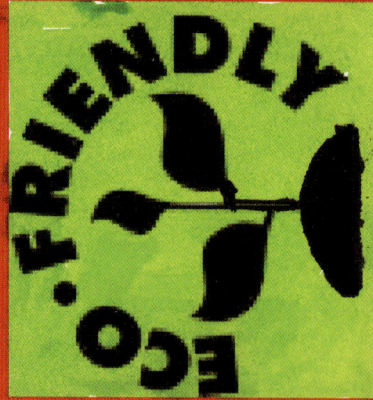

ECO FRIENDLY

Harrie Wheatley Yr 6
Thorne Brooke Primary School Doncaster

24

Noviolence

Ban all of these

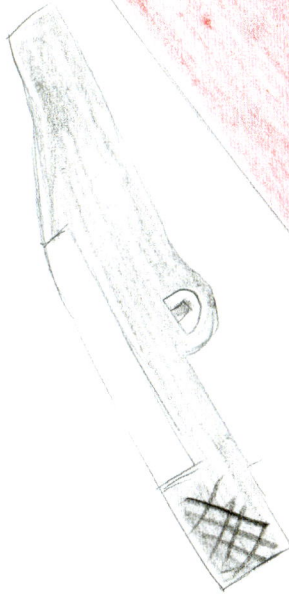

cigarettes

bombs

bullets

Knives

drugs

guns

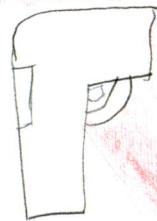

Leona McManus. Limegrove School. Age 12.

Leona McManus aged 12
Limegrove School Limavady

Timothy Durbin and Christian Clifford

NO CHILD ABUSE!

KILL GUNS NOT PEOPLE

NO FIREARMS!

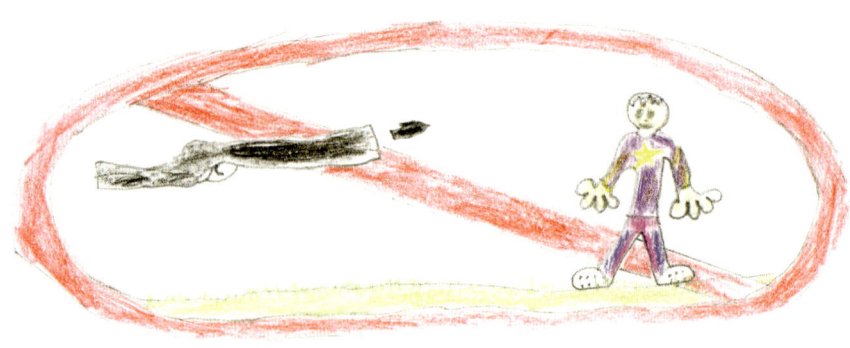

Tim Durbin, Christian Clifford aged 10
Longwick C of E Combined School Bucks

More Wind Turbines

Albert McDonald aged 15
Limegrove School Limavady

guns are bad!
Ban guns
Forever

STOP WAR IN IRAQ!!!

NO WAR!

Did you know?
The war in Iraq
cost...
$457,104,156,735
Rising rapidly

William Harrison, Alistair Bee aged 9
Longwick C of E Combined School Bucks

28

Pick up Litter and throw it away

Work together

Only be kind

Respect others

Learn from your mistaks

Do your best

Peace

Equally Unique

Always Show Kindnes

Ceaful what you do

Everyone is unique

WORLD

A BETTER PLACE

MAKE OUR WORLD

Give Racism the red card

Donate

Money AND Clothes

James Savage
St Aidan's Catholic Primary School Merseyside

Get clean water to people who need it

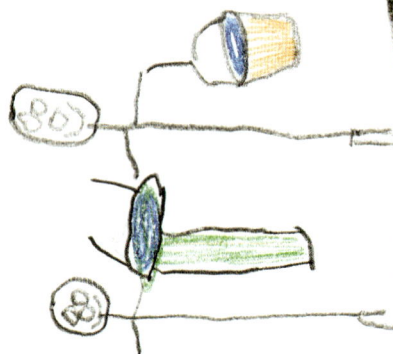

Martin Falls aged 15
Limegrove School Limavady

GLOBAL WARMING!!

Emily Boulton aged 10
Castle Primary School Somerset

CHILD CRUELTY

THE RESPECT RAP

We have to stop child cruelty
Because its really bad.
Children should be shown respect
Otherwise they will be sad.

This is what we don't want to happen. Do you?

Mike Toole, Jack Grey aged 10
Longwick C of E Combined School Bucks

32

ECO WORLD

Marc Miller aged 9
Canmore Primary School Dunfermline

Padraig
I think we should stop having wars
because people get killed.

Padraig Marshall
Fleming Fulton School
Belfast

Padraig Marshall aged 10
Fleming Fulton School Belfast

Get clean water to people who need it

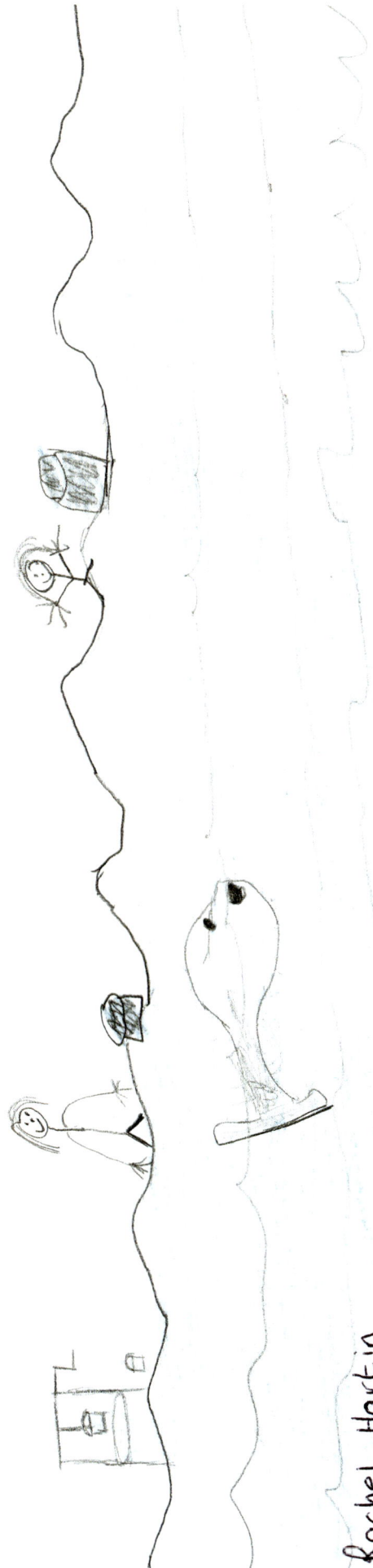

Rachel Hartin
Limegrove School   Age 15.

Rachel Hartin aged 15
Limegrove School Limavady

STOP ANIMAL CRUELTY!

— this should be this —

What is Animal Abuse?

"stopping animal cruelty makes the world a better place!"

A. Animal cruelty can be lots of different things that are harmful to animals from neglect to killing. Intentional cruelty is taking away from an animal. food, shelter, socialization, water, not taking it the vets or killing it

Force-Fed Animal Abuse

Ducks and Geese are forced-fed unnaturally large amounts of food through a metal tube that is shoved down their throats 2 or 3 times a day. The regular overfeeding causes their livers to become diseased. The livers become enlarged up to 10 times it's normal size, making it difficult for it to move and for it to even walk.

help me

Lauren Durrant, Liana Rosewell aged 10
Longwick C of E Combined School Bucks

Sophie Hurst
J5

Save Our
Planet

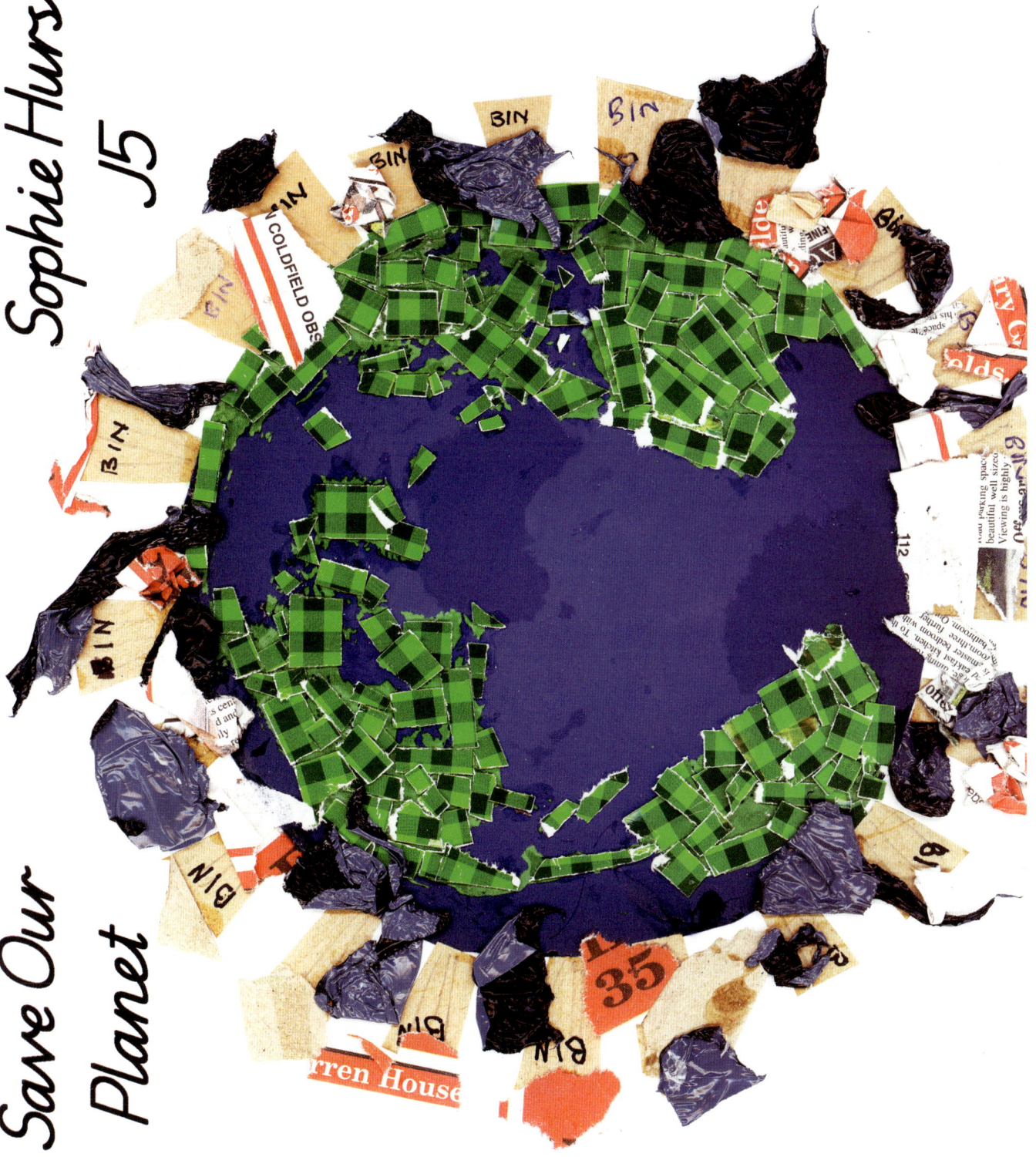

Sophie Hurst Yr 6
Highclare School Birmingham

37

Pollution Beware!

You're in for a SCARE!

don't be a dummy to think it's Funny!

One way of stoping poullution is to stop driving and stop factoures. So heres some of my idies to stop it from hapning.

In most touns we should have a battery pourened train going round toun picking up children up and taking them to there schools. Also they should gine swreets out for being good and then put there wrappers in the recycle box next to it. When the battries run out you must recycle it and buy a new one.

Be a litter bug – AND YOU'RE FINED!

You are being watched.

by Jane

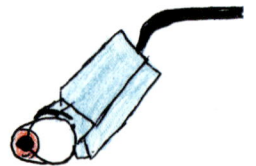

Jane
Coates Lane Primary School Lancashire

'GANGS' 'WARS' CHANGE
'LAWS' 'RACISM'

Rosie
Haynes
Year 5
age 9
Braunston C.E
School

We need to change,
This world is at the brink.
If we don't, oh if we don't
Soon we will go in a blink.

We need to change,
Soon we will die,
See what the public thinks,
Don't pass the chance by.

We need to change
This is a deadline.
oh, oh, oh, oh, oooh,
Take this as a sighn

Be more like
Princess Diana

Rosie Haynes aged 9
Braunston C.E. School Daventry

MAKE LOVE NOT WAR

Small things still
Count so listen to us,
Stop Bullying Now!

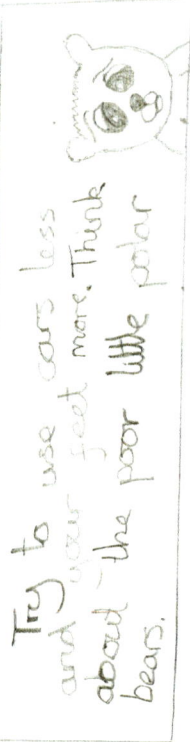

Every three seconds a
child dies, 1...2...3.
Shall we stop this.....Now!

NO MORE Racism!

Cruel

Try to use cars less
and wear feet more. Think
about the poor little polar
bears.

Helping Stop

Cruelty

BIG
things isn't a
little thing

A Pet
is for
life not
just for
christmas

Fran Furniss, Laura Pennell aged 10
Longwick C of E Combined School Bucks

NO WAR!

If you stop making guns you could stop war there will be world peace.

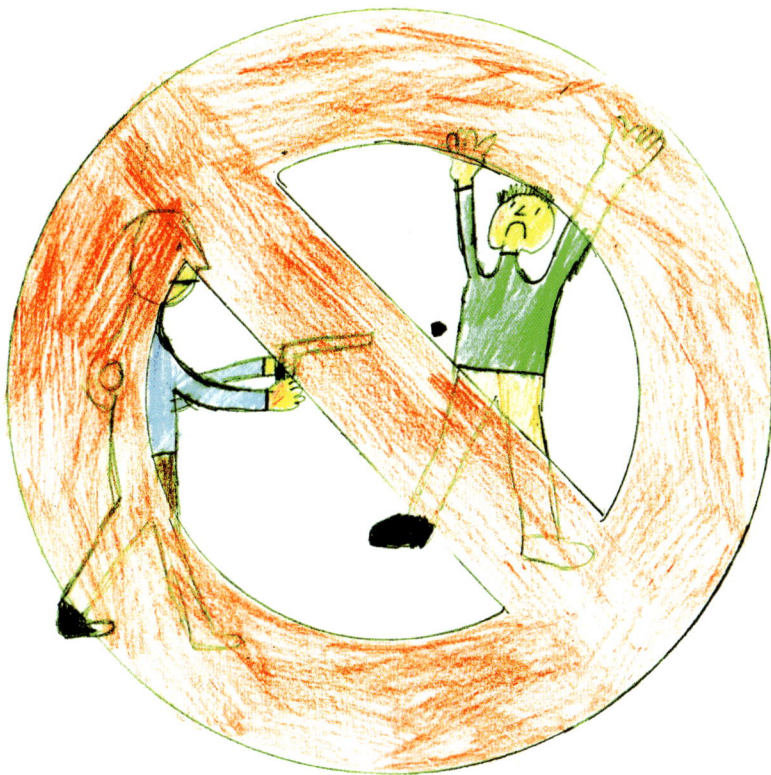

This is the right way to live.

Tom Monaghan aged 10
Castle Primary School Somerset

IMPROVING THE WORLD!

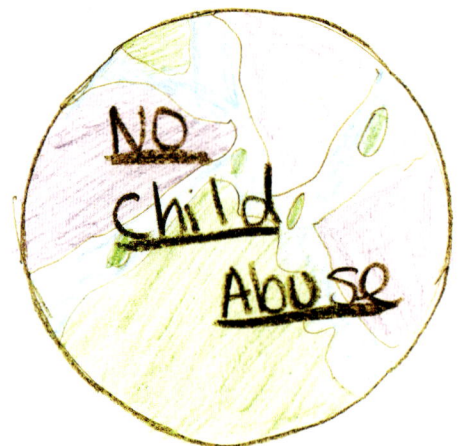

No Graffiti

No Bullying

The World

No Litter

No Child Abuse

Yasmin Iqbal aged 10
Hawthorns Junior School Lancashire

Name Rebecca Whitelaw   Age 14

Date 06/11/07

How would you like to change the world?

① People should help each other more.

② Create more charities to help people.

③ Recycle more - Global warming - look after our environment

Draw a picture of how you would change the world.

Balance the Worlds Scales

Jobs
Food
Drink
Money
Medicine's
Water
Joy

Poor
Thirst
Famine
Drought
Sadness
Disease
Death

Elizabeth Greenwell aged 9
St Margaret of Scotland Catholic Junior School Luton

If you cause pollution,
By driving and dumping your waste,
Save energy that's the solution,
Anything else is bad in taste!

So everybody please say **STOP**,
If you don't our world will turn old,
If you don't the world will go pop,
Please listen you have been told!

Our planet earth will get so hot,
The ozone layer has a hole,
So please look after what we've got,
Saving the world is our **GOAL!**

By Hannah chandler
Age:9

Hannah Chandler aged 9
St Cecilia's Catholic Primary School Surrey

45

AND REMEMBER PICK UP YOUR DOGS DROPPINGS!

Walk your dog

Meet other dogs on the way!

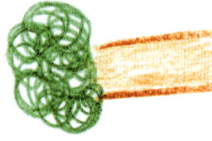

Save your planet!
Save your world
Save your roads
Save your money
Save your dog!

Give your dog some fresh air, exercise and to go to the toilet.

Jasmine Webb
Braunston C.E. School Daventry

46

IF THE WORLD COULD CHANGE THE WORLD IT'S YOUR WORLD USE IT ABUSE IT DON'T IT

Care for one another
help every other
always put on a smile
never bully anyone
give generously
every one is equal

trust & honesty
have faith in outher
enjoy your life

welcome outhers
our lives our
realise our
love our planet
dont harm outhers
! *!
! 4 ever .

If I could change the world.
I would Stop Guns.
And make more buns.
Make prisons tough
keep them in hand cuffs
Those killers out Here
Beware our world
Make our world safe
Happy and people who
And pray for you are missing

This is what we want
what I want
not we what want

Emma O Hagan yr 6
St Aidan's Catholic Primary School Merseyside

I would like people to have

better cars for the environment. The smoke

is bad.

bad

super

Padraig Magee aged 10
Fleming Fulton School Belfast

Improving the world we live in

Protecting endangered animals,
Should be the first thing on your mind,
People need to know,
That they should always be kind.

Having no gun crime,
Would make the world better,
Stop all the gun crimes,
And stop wasting BLOOD!

Giving money to charity,
Help us now,
Don't ask why,
And don't ask how.

Use water carefully,
Don't waste it there,
Watch how you use it,
Always use it with care.

NO POLLUTION!
Please help us,
When we try to stop,
We recycle to help.

Graffiti has to stop,
It is very bad,
Wish nobody would do it,
It makes people sad.

Stop being a litter bug,
Littering is pollution.
When people drop a drug,
Never pick it up.

Recycling is best,
To save the poor little trees,
Please help us now,
We are down on our knees.

Have more houses,
So people are happy,
They can have a place to live,
Where it makes you snappy.

To behave well,
Is to set a good example,
When you work hard at school,
Then you have good friends and be cool.

Bolaji and Zahrah, aged 10,
West Twyford Primary School, London

Make Britain Better

Make Britain greener by changing lots of things.
Make the world better
by doing lots of things
The crazy drug dealers
are slimy little snakes
Graffiti is terrible
people hate it
so much.
Recycle
lots
of
things
to make
the world
good. Smoking is
for babies. It's very
very bad. Littering is also
very very bad. So why do
people do it if it's very bad
So now that's almost saved the World!

Ryan Smith, aged 10,
Thornwood Primary School, Glasgow

How to save the earth

This is our acrostic poem

Recycle – you should do.
Electricity – you should save.
Clean up litter – that we should not throw.
Yellow – the colour the sun <u>should</u> be.
Care for our world and you will have a happy life.
Life that should not be polluted.
Earth is being polluted every hour of the day.

Frank Hills, **Jake Taylor**, year 6,
Thorne Brooke Primary School, Doncaster

What do we have?

The bombs that drop,
The people that cry,
The only question is
Who will die?

As she surrenders,
through her own fate,
she knows whats coming
and its far from great.

The knife is drew
from beneath the pocket
and all that's alive
is a golden locket.

Inside that locket
was her joy and pride
a little boy gleaming
with his mum by his side.

So what do we have?
With a world full of danger
Well, Ill tell you
a world with me, as a stranger.

My dream world
is for happiness all round
no bombs, guns or knives
so then we can be found.

and as she closes the curtains
and rests on her bed
she has her dream world
bubbling inside her head.

MAKE IT HAPPEN

Chelsea Tramiro, aged 10,
St Margaret of Scotland Catholic
Junior School, Luton

Close to Home

I want a world in which children can be free to go round the block by themselves. I get quite scared because there are lots of stories in the newspaper about children being attacked. Children in the past could go around on their own but now they have to have parents to protect them. I wish I was not scared any more.

Rebecca Hupp, aged 10,
St George's School for Girls, Edinburgh

GUNS KILL, KILL GUNS

There are a 1000 people killed in the world each day from gun crime.

59% of the world's population own a gun.

Could you be in danger?

Don't we deserve to live in a safer world?
What are your children carrying?

Can we persuade the criminals to give up their guns for a safer future?

Let's Kill the Guns before they kill You!!

St Sebastian's C of E Primary School
Berks

How would you improve the World you live in?

I think a future without gas or electricity would be very scary and therefore I would improve our World by asking our Government to fund the research into clean coal technology (CCT). Before I was born, people used coal to heat their homes and it was also used for making gas and electricity but, because it was dirty, we stopped using it.

However, this coal is still under our country and seas and there are now ways of cleaning it up by removing CO_2 from it and storing this deep underground. This process is know as "carbon capture and storage" (CCS). The rest of the World could then learn about this from us, especially countries like India and China who still burn "dirty" coal which harms our environment with greenhouse emissions.

Also I think more education is needed about recycling and saving electricity and water. Lots of public buildings (including schools) have lights and heating on whether they are needed or not – this should be against the law.

Daniella Jones,
Highclare School, Birmingham

A BETTER PLACE

This is a beautiful place
We are ruining its great face.

Try not to cause so much pollution
Fewer factories are the only solution.

Not so much graffiti on the walls
It costs too much to repaint for all.

When war was invented it tore us apart
It causes so much sadness in your heart.

There should be peace in this great place,
Love for the entire human race.

Let peace on earth prevail,
And let the flags of freedom sail.

Reece Crawford, aged 9,
Canmore Primary School, Dunfermline

World Wreckers

I want to get this message to you

Whether you're an elephant or a kangaroo

It's wrecking our world

Pollution has curled

And this disaster is coming from who?

Every human, every car

Makes an impact, oooarh

There is no reason coming to me

Why we should live in a fantasy.

Many people push this aside

That in some years we'll live in the tide.

Water is growing, land is drowning

And it's affecting us all.

Jenny Ansell, year 6,
Braunston CE Primary School, Daventry

Global Getaway!

A summer morning, a beautiful day.
Thinking nothing can stand in its way,
The dancing trees, shimmering in the breeze,
A smiling countryside, totally at ease.

But now, it's all falling out of our grasp.

A summer morning, misty and grey,
Giving up hope just running away,
The wilting trees, stooping in the dust,
The countryside, save it we must.

The sea blue sky, dances by
Enjoying the soft winds lullaby
The confident cliffs stand proud and strong
Listening to a beautiful bird's song.

But now it's all slipping out of reach

The stone grey sky, stuck so high
Hearing rough winds shrieking by
The crumbling cliff feeble and weak
Veiled in the misty air, dark and bleak.

We don't want our skies mirky and grey
This really is a global getaway!

ACT NOW!!

"It was a beautiful day when I wrote this poem. I hate the thought that the magic of nature could just disappear if we do not look after the world."

Constance Heathfield, Year 6,
Rodborough Primary School, Stroud

How would I improve the world I live in.

Every child should be involved
in a loving family.
Loving, caring
appreciated.

Every child has the right to live
in a house
whether black or white.
A warm, cosy, comfy home
with clean water and food.

Every child has the right to have a home
With a bed,
comfortable,
bouncy and soft.

Every home should have a bathroom
with a bath, sink,
shower and toilet.

That home that they live in
should be solid.
It should be made secure
from brick, wood or stone.

That home made of brick, wood or stone
should have a kitchen.
A kitchen complete with knives, forks,
bowls, pots and pans
and most importantly
fresh food and clean water.

That is how I would improve the World.

Sam Owen, aged 9,
Clun Primary School, Neath

Greener Britain

Why why does the world have vandals?
Why why does the world have thieves?
Why why do people in the world take drugs?
Why why does the world have needs?
Why why do people litter and pollute the sea?
Why why do people kill the animals that live in the sea?

Jack Sinclair, aged 10,
Thornwood Primary School, Glasgow

Earth's Dream of Peace

This is earth talking:

I have a dream – a dream of no wars,
weapons or armies. I want world
peace! YES! YES! YES!

No bombs that fall and kill the
innocent – no guns that shoot and
cause tears to fall.

No hatred that makes men evil and
unkind to their brothers.
I want world peace! YES! YES! YES!

Matthew Campbell, aged 9,
Canmore Primary, Dunfermline

The magic box

I will put in my box
An eclipse from a summer night,
the fire from a Japanese dragon,
sparks from an electric fish,
and a flash of lightening awakening
the large sky.

I will put in the box
The spring of an Australian kangaroo,
A shout off my little brother and a
show from the colours of the rainbow.

I will put in the box
Three wishes spoken in Gaelic,
a last finishing move from a wrestler,
a last slide from the world's greatest
skier.

My box is made from
Gold and silver stars,
purple silk, and soft purple feathers.

I shall bobsleigh on my box on a journey of the great French mountains.

Reece Rigby, aged 11,
Moorfield Primary School, Cheshire

we throw lots of paper
we burn lots of wood
we really don't recycle as much as we should
whales and creatures living in the sea
don't take them all just for your tea!
too much fishing is cruel and wrong
if we fish too much they won't last long
REDUCE, RE-USE, RECYCLE, REFUSE
that's the rhyme that we should use
it's over here, it's over there
rubbish is almost everywhere
everyone recycle don't be shy
its not that hard, give it a try
the whole world knows that's
how it goes
there's lots of water
there's lots of land
and some of it is covered with sand
that is why we must be alert
because this disaster we must avert.

Brogan Riley, aged 9,
Coates Lane Primary School, Lancashire

Save the world

The little circle
Is full of big things inside
Seek and you will find

Inspiring things
Making you comfortable
As if your own home

But something quite dark
Is getting closer to you
Sensing death and sin

Polluting your world
Leaving it in such a state
Your world is at risk

The world is at risk
Hope. The sky is the limit
Please make the right choice

Haiku – **Claudia Afranie**,
St Cecilia's Catholic Primary School, Surrey

 everybody  who  needs **A** a

 wheelchair sh∼ should  have **1** one

Rachael

Rachael Rice aged 10
Fleming Fulton School Belfast

I hate the wars in Iraq. The screaming voices of mothers with their children, running in and out of wrecked buildings looking for a safe place to rest. The shouting of orders and commands coming from the General to retreat. The missile like bombs that blow up the city walls and let the enemies in. The fights in the street over leadership. All this has to be changed for the good of everyone. To make the fighting stop the governments all over the world must work together and help Iraq regain leadership over their own country.

Alice Cullen, aged 10,
St George's School for Girls, Edinburgh

Bully – A Play

Characters
Danielle: singer
Ashleigh: friend
Leanne: friend
Louise: bully

Chapter 1 : (*At school*)
Ashleigh   What shall we do today?
Leanne   I don't … (*gets interrupted by Louise*)
Louise (*cocky*)   I will tell you what to do today!
Leanne   Leave us alone!
Louise   NO!
Ashleigh   Will you two stop fighting.

Chapter 2:
(*Danielle dances in*)
Danielle   What's up you guys?
All of them   HER! (*All blame it on each other*)
Danielle   Do you want me to show you's something?
All of them   YES!
Danielle (*sings*)   How can we make the world a better place, treat others nicely don't laugh in their face, never be nasty, never be mean, always be friends, so go catch your dreams
Louise   Whatever.
Ashleigh   Yeah (*storms off dragging feet along floor*)
Danielle   What's with those two?

Chapter 3: (*Two days later back at school*)
Ashleight   We're sorry, we want to be friends. (*in a lonely voice*)
Leanne/Danielle   Friends.
Ashleigh/Louise   Friends.

THE END!

Lauren Hand, Chelsea Boyer, Rachel Pond, Bianca Georgiadis,
Thorne Brooke Primary School, Doncaster

THE APPRECIATION OF THE CREATION

It was Monday morning,
When God decided,
To make a place full of love and good,
So that's what he created.

He gave that place a name,
Which we know as the world,
But do we all know how it started?
Well now you're going to be told.

At first the world was empty,
Did not have any light,
But then Gods spirits moved over the waters,
And he said "let the world" be bright.

Then he separated the waters,
From below and above,
And in between was heaven,
Where came the white dove.

Then he took the water below heaven,
And divided it in two,
One half earth and one half sea,
But on that day there was more that he went to do.

On that day he said,
"Make plants bearing seed,
And trees bearing fruit"
And that was something that the world did need.

Then it was the forth day,
And in heaven God put lights,
To shine on the earth,
And separate the days from nights.

Next God made creatures,
To live in the sea and the sky,
He blessed them all and said,
"Be fruitful and multiply."

Next he made creatures of all kind,
And in the image of him made men,
Then God saw everything he'd made,
And gave it a ten out of ten.

Now it was the seventh day,
And God spent it in relaxation,
It was the last day of the week,
And the last day of the creation.

So remember all of that effort,
That God put in,
And try to make the world a better place,
Like to throw things in the recycle bin.

Anna Moloney, aged 10,
St Cecilia's Catholic Primary School, Surrey

A Song –
to the tune of 'Baa Baa Black Sheep'

What's the future
Will we still drive cars?
No sir, No sir, No sir, No sir
Pollution kills the stars!

Pollution, pollution
We hate all the pollution
If we get rid of it we'll save our town!

What's the future
Will we still fly planes?
No sir, No sir, No sir, No sir
Gas can give you pain!

Gas, gas, gas, gas
We hate all the Gas
If we get rid of it we'll save our town!

What's the future
Will we still eat chips
No sir, No sir, No sir, No sir
Littering stops the ships!

Littering, littering
We hate all the littering
If we get rid of it we'll save our town!

What's the future
Will we still have trains?
No sir, No sir, No sir, No sir
Unless we use our brains!

Hey!!

Year 6,
Thorne Brooke Primary School, Doncaster
**Shannon Holland, Megan Welsh, Nicole Myers,
Morgan Murphy, Jordan Young, Lauren Millen,
Melissa Smith, Scarlett Britian, Courtney McNelis**

LITTER

Litter everywhere
In the park or in the street,
Trying to clean it up
To make the world a better place,
Eco friendly we should be for
Rubbish harms our world.

Emma Robertson, aged 9,
Canmore Primary School, Dunfermline

Life?

Gunshots ringing out
Never ceasing to end
Neither does the
Loss of life
Why?

Roaming creatures
Living and free
Yet we kill them
For one of their unique features
Why?

Every thirty seconds
An innocent human being
Weak and exhausted
Dies of starvation
Why?

Bottles smash
Lunged into the shadowy darkness
Blood trickles out
Of the victims body
Why?

Trees shrivel
Cowering in fear
From the siege
Of acid rain
Why?

A dolphin rides the waves
Until it sees a floating plastic bag
It swallows it, chokes on it,
And slowly dies.
Why?

A lion freely roams
The savanna until it hears a gunshot
It runs
Too late
Why does this happen?
Why? Why? Why?
ACT NOW!

*"I am concerned that everything is
dying around me. We don't value life
enough. Governments have got to
do something now to save the world."*

Joe Ferguson, year 6,
Rodborough Primary School, Stroud

One day there was a little girl called Sophie.

Sophie, one day was walking to school freely breathing in lots of car fumes. Every car was just letting lots of car fumes into the air because it was a very cold day, and they were warming up their cars.

When Sophie finally got to school, she didn't feel very well at all. Sophie went to her teacher called Miss Whatly and said

"Miss I don't feel very well." Sophie mumbled.

"Well, see how you feel after lunch, if you don't feel better, then go and call your mum, see what she says." Miss Whatly said.

So it came to lunch time and Sophie wasn't feeling better than before.

She went to the office and said,
"Im not feeling well at all, and my teacher told me to come and call my mum." She said trying not to say it loud enough for other students to hear. The person who Sophie told then let her call her mum.

"Mum." Sophie mumbled.
"I don't feel well at all and I can't breathe very well."

"Ok, I'll come and get you now." Sophie's mum said.

So half an hour later Sophie was lying on the sofa with a blanket over her drinking a cup of hot chocolate.

"Can you think of anything that could have caused it?" Sophie's mum said.

"Well, it could have been because I breathed in car fumes, this morning." Sophie said, just audible.

"WHAT." Sophie's mum bellowed.

"How could you do this?" Her mum said trying as hard as she could to calm down.
"We have to go to the doctors, right now." Sophie's mum said.

At the doctors Sophie had to tell the doctor all the truth.
Then after all the questioning the doctor said "Well I think the best thing to do is to have a few days at home, to try and recover." The doctor told Sophie and her mum.

So a week went by with Sophie at home and she finally said to her mum "On Monday can I try and go back to school?".

"Well lets see how you are feeling, ok."

Monday came and Sophie was feeling as good as new and from then on she was more careful about what she breathed in.

The moral of this story is that car fumes are bad for your health and something needs to be done. We're not saying that nobody can have a car, but we think people should find something different to petrol. E.G. vegetable oil. We hope that you will take this into account. Thank you for reading our story.

Robert Fayolle, Tom Shaw, Callum McGready, aged 9,
Budbrooke Primary School, Warwick

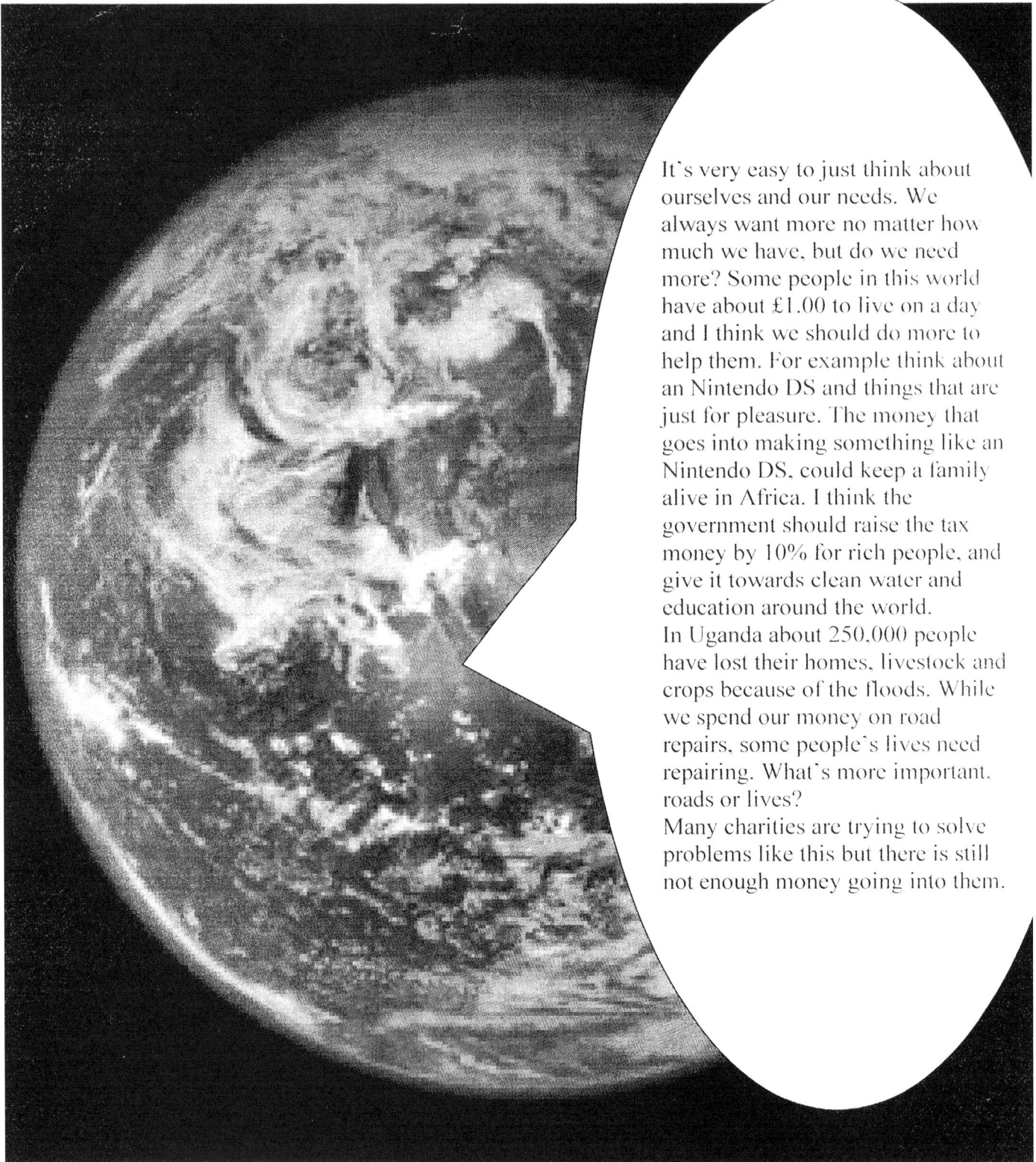

It's very easy to just think about ourselves and our needs. We always want more no matter how much we have, but do we need more? Some people in this world have about £1.00 to live on a day and I think we should do more to help them. For example think about an Nintendo DS and things that are just for pleasure. The money that goes into making something like an Nintendo DS, could keep a family alive in Africa. I think the government should raise the tax money by 10% for rich people, and give it towards clean water and education around the world.

In Uganda about 250.000 people have lost their homes, livestock and crops because of the floods. While we spend our money on road repairs, some people's lives need repairing. What's more important, roads or lives?

Many charities are trying to solve problems like this but there is still not enough money going into them.

Anna Marsden Yr 6
St Sebastian's C of E Primary School Berks

THE EARTH IS A LIGHT

My earth is like a light
It shines so very bright,
The sun makes me feel glad
It does not make me sad.

Earth must be peaceful
Earth must be good,
Laughter and light
Gives me so much might.

Earth should be good place
Peace and friendship for all,
Earthlings must be a shining race
Lights that shine and embrace.

Catherine Bullions, aged 9,
Canmore Primary School, Dunfermline

Save our World

Help! Save our world
We need to stop polluting
Stop! Stop! Some factories
Help! Help! Get more recycling bins
Stop! Stop! Dropping litter
Help! Help! Sell more diesel
Stop! Stop! Leaving the engine on.

Please Please
Save our World
Please Please
Save our World

Help! Save our world
We need all your help
Stop! Stop! Vandalising
Help! Help! Please help
Stop! Stop! Starting fires
Help! Help! Someone may die

!!!STOP POLLUTING NOW!!!

Nadia Stewart, aged 10,
Thornwood Primary School, Glasgow

How I would improve the world

I would improve the schools in other countries by giving them more money to buy books, pens and maybe uniforms to make all the children the same and make them feel that they are part of one big family that will protect them.

Why can't we all get along in the world? Does it matter that other children have different skin colour? Does it matter that their religion is different to mine?

I would fine anyone who drops their rubbish on the ground where I live and play and dumps their rubbish in our rivers. These people are naughty and lazy.

I would improve the love and care in the world. I would love every child in every part of the world to have parents like mine because then they will feel protected, loved and comforted.

I would help all the horrible people in the world to become better parents by showing them how to care and love.

I would improve all children's rights in all the different countries of my world.

That's what I would improve in the world.

Jade Davies, aged 9,
Clun Primary School, Neath

Dear Lord

I know I don't often talk to you, but at least that means I don't ask you for very much,
But now something has come up which I really need your help with – right now.
I knew a lovely man and as far as I can tell he always tried to be good.
But being good didn't seem to help him.
Neither did him being as tall and as strong as a great oak, nor did his years of playing rugby,
When cancer took hold of his body.
He died too early – he even missed his favourite rugby team winning the league,
I know he was quite old but I also know that there are thousands of
others dying young from cancer and other diseases,
And I am sure many of them were good people and don't deserve their fate,
Nobody on earth seems to know the cure to cancer, so I thought I would ask you to tell somebody,
Apparently you made the world so you must know how to cure it,
Anyway I thought it was worth a try.
Oh and by the way I will keep tyring to be good.

PS The man was my Grandad

Siobhan Croall,
Collis Primary School, Middlesex

Why do people?

Why do people kidnap children?
It makes everyone in the world depressed.
I wish it wouldn't happen,
It would make society less stressed.

Why do people kill animals,
Like leopards, tigers and polar bears?
I'd much rather see them in their natural habitat,
Than being a rug on the stairs.

Why do people drive their vehicles,
When they know it causes pollution?
Everyone should do more cycling and walking,
It keeps you fit and healthy and is the ideal solution.

Why do people leave their T.V. and computers on standby,
When they go out in the morning?
Don't they realise that be turning them off,
It would help to reduce global warming.

Beth Thomson, aged 9,
St Cecilia's Catholic Primary School, Surrey

WORLD PEACE

Everyone must be eco friendly.
Everyone must respect each other's rights.
Everyone has the right to be cared for.
Everyone has the right to an education.
Everyone has the right to have clean water.
Everyone has the right to have food.
No child must be forced to join the army or take part in a war.
Everyone has the right to have his or her own opinion.
No one under 18 is allowed to drink alcohol.
No one under 16 should smoke.
There should be no bullying.
No one under 17 should be driving.
No bad language should be said.
There should not be any fighting.
There should not be anyone that is polluting.
Everyone should be taking care of our world.
Be responsible of the things that you have.
No one under 18 is allowed to go to the elk.
Never steal things that are not yours.
No one has the right to tease other people.
No one should ever be setting fire to other people's houses.
People should never be shooting people or police men.
People should go to jail for shooting or setting fires.

Patrick McCrystal,
St Brigid's Primary School, N Ireland

Happy days up on the common

Happy days up on the common eating delicious winstones ice cream whipped
to perfection.
Happy days up on the common with the howling wind blowing me from side to side.
Happy days up on the common running down the dippy dillies.
Happy days up on the common where rosy faced families walk their dogs.
Happy days up on the common where teletubbies come to play.
Happy days up on the common where my little sister runs riot!
Happy days up on the common, memories and a precious world which we must always
treasure.

"I want the common, which I love, to stay the way it is and not ever be destroyed."

Jake Church, year 6,
Rodborough Primary School, Stroud

Helping poorer countries

I think poorer countries should have at least half of what we have and we should not be so selfish and greedy. Poorer countries should have money like us, food, clothes and proper houses and lots more. Imagine if we were the poor country and had no food. We would not like it. They should not be starving to death and if they get ill there's no doctors. They should be helped. Save poorer countries.

Megan Wickins, aged 10,
Lavant House School, Chichester

One Little Girl

One little girl
All on her own
Sat in a cupboard
With no home

One little girl
Crying her heart out
No one there for help
When the gunshots shout

One little girl
Wandering round and
round
Wondering where she is
As she has not been found

One little girl
Life ebbing away
A victim of starvation
Pleading for salvation

One little girl
No life, no hope
Just debris and destruction
Death and destruction
The gifts of war

"I wrote this poem after talking to my nan about the war. I want to grow up in peace and happiness."

Katie Ashforth-Shaw, year 6,
Rodborough Primary School,
Stroud

How to make our world a better place

To make our world a better place do this:

Pick up any rubbish that you see on the roads or streets, you wouldn't drop rubbish in your own home so don't do it here.
Reuse plastic bags. E.g. If you use a plastic bag once in Tesco's use it over again. People all over the world keep their plastic bags stashed somewhere in their homes so reuse them.
Save pollution and walk to either school or work or even use your bicycle. There is too much pollution in our world so start walking its also good exercise.
Don't fight with anyone make the world a non-fightable place to live. People are getting killed and badly injured so STOP the fighting.
Plant more nice things like trees, flowers and maybe fruit. If you like eating fruit plant yourself a FRUIT tree.
Make our food packaging smaller. Have you seen the size of our food its small compared to the packages?
If your child is bored or you're bored maybe build more family places to spend time together. We all get bored so go out and DON'T drive there walk there.
Take your pet out for a walk every now and again. If you have a pet what's the point in having it when you don't spend time with it.

I hope these things are good enough to make our world a better place to live in!!!

Rachel Kelly,
Hart Memorial Primary School, N Ireland

HOW I THINK WE COULD IMPROVE OUR WORLD ......

Ronan Karicos
St Brigid's Primary School N Ireland

This should be.....

this

Child Poverty

A little girl, the age of four,
Sits in the gutter all alone.

She sobs, she crys, she weeps
As she begs, people ignore
The lonely child, battered and bruised.
As night falls the cold sweeps in.
The rats bite and gnaw,
But as morning breaks there is no more
Of the little girl who died...age four.

Every child should feel happy

WE CAN STOP THIS HAPPENING BY GIVING CHILDREN HOMES AND PROVIDING FOOD FOR A SMALL DONATION TO HELP CHILDREN SURVIVE!

Children don't deserve this

Charlotte Mann aged 10
Longwick C of E Combined School Bucks

66

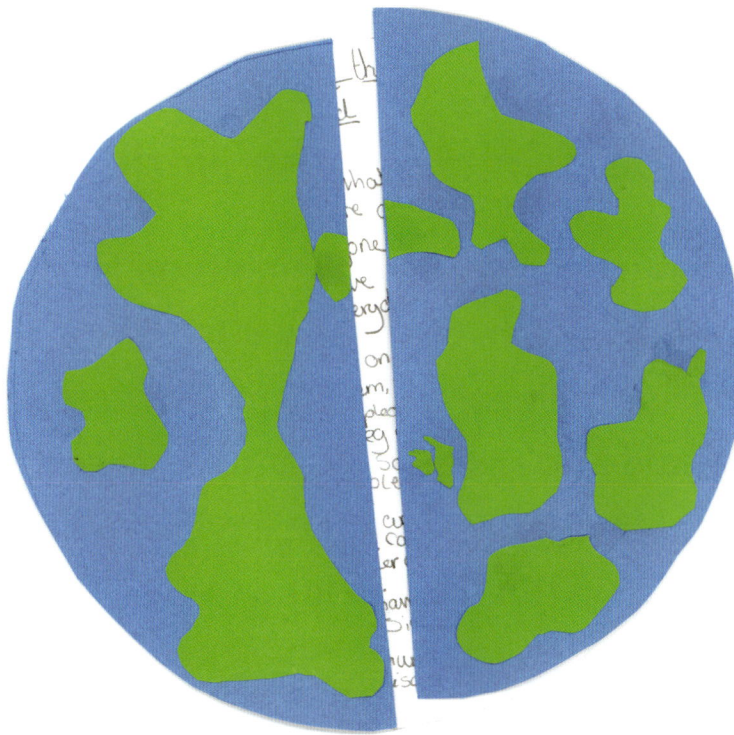

Saving the World

1. Look around what do you see
pollution everywhere also under the sea
So to help everyone
Just do what we say
recycle nearly everyday

2. Starving Children on the street
no one to help them, nothing to eat
So help them please
or they will beg on there knees
So give them some money
Please please please

3. people hunt animals for there fur
It's not very fair cause we just don't care.
What about thier children
they will die.
if they don't have their Mum right by
there side.

by Hannah Gunn Charlotte Spalding
and Mellisa Mastertin

Hannah Gunn, Charlotte Spalding, Mellisa Mastertin
St George's School for Girls Edinburgh

67

How would you improve the world we live in?

If it was up to me, I would stop all pollution in the world. Also I would stop climate change by 80 percent. I would do this by making it illegal to use so many chemicals in factories. I would also make it illegal to have really big chimneys that blow smoke into the environment. I think that this would help the world a lot.

By Bradley Webb

Bradley Webb
ISP Teynham Primary School Teynham

Poh the Little Inuit

In the North pole lived Poh the Inuit. Poh loved the North pole because he was born there. When people went to the North pole they felt sorry for Poh because the ice was melting. In the year 2020 most of the ice caps where gone. By the year 2030 Poh was dead because the ice melted, he drowned.

The reason Poh died in the end was because of global warming. It wasn't caused by one person it was caused by everyone in the world we live in. That won't happen in your life time and it may not happen in our life time but it will happen in someones life time so lets take care of Our beautiful World!

Natasha Duffy
St George's School for Girls Edinburgh

Put A Wind Turbine in the Sea

Put a wind turbine in the Sea
no one will complain
Put a wind turbine in the Sea
Save energy for the World

They cost money but our world will last longer.

Georgia Leggott Yr 5
Thorne Brooke Primary School Doncaster

Georgia Leggott Yr 5
Thorne Brooke Primary School Doncaster

71

Re-cycling one tin saves enough energy to power a T.V. for three hours

Up to 60% of rubbish can be re-cycled

But if made easier people might re-cycle more

Britain could be filled with rubbish in only 8 months

If we re-cycle, our children will have better lives

Should we take money off bills for good re-cycling?

How can we do the right thing?

By Jack Walmsley St. Sebastians

Jack Walmsley
St Sebastian's C of E Primary School Berks

How to change the world

How have we made the world so bad?
How have we made the people so sad?
How is the world just so doomed?
How have we given it such a big wound?

Why don't we see just what this could be
And examine what kind of destroyers are we
Do we have hope in our future life?
Dare we look past this current strife

How you can save the world

You can save the world by doing the following...

• Save paper.
• Take a shower insted of a bath.
• Plant a plant everytime you go on a long journey in a vheicle.
• If you are going to drive somewhere that is only a short distance walk insted.
• Recycle in and out of school.
• Do not leave the tap on while you are brushing your teeth.
• Do not drop litter on the floor.

by Elin
Pembrey

Elin Pembrey aged 10
Castle Primary School Somerset

73

How would you improve the world you live in?

Looking after animals

Please look after the animals
I will sing a hymn
They're only tiny fishes
With small little fins

Innocent little fishes
Swimming in the sea
Soon they're served on dishes
Ready for my tea
Together we can help them
You and me!

By Bronte Harvey
(9)

Bronte Harvey
Lavant House Chichester

74

The ice cap on Mount Kilimanjaro could be completely gone by 2025. More than 80 percent of the ice field has disappeared since the mountain was first mapped in 1912.

STOP POLLUTION

AS THE SEA ICE GOES-SO DO THE POLAR BEARS

When you throw away plastic it takes over 300 years to reabsorbed, so recycle!

Guy Molony
Collis Primary School Middlesex

I woulike to Ane chilwrens hous. to make them lovely

BABY
BABY

Rianna

Rianna Jackson aged 10
Fleming Fulton School Belfast

How to improve our world

The wind is blowing
And soon it will be snowing
and people will be throwing
litter on the ground
I'ts Just so Sad
And really really bad

Loads of little fishes swimming in the sea
please help save them with me
don't eat them for your tea
Just put them back in the sea

Poem by Rhiannon Phelps
(9)

Rhiannon Phelps aged 9
Lavant House Chichester

A Message To the World

All the people of the planet,
Global warming - we should ban it!
Stop cutting down all the trees,
And recycle paper please!

The animals are dying,
And everybody's crying.
But don't just sit and stare-
Do something about this scare!

Turn off the lights,
When they're not in use,
Recycle what you can,
RECYCLE, RE-USE, REDUCE!

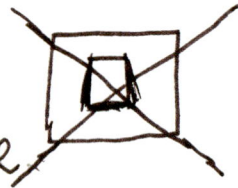

RECYCLE-SAVE OUR PLANET!

Charlotte Fraser-High
St George's School for Girls Edinburgh

IMPROVING OUR FUTURE WORLD

PEACE

GOOD ATTITUDE

PROGRESS CHANGE

ENVIRONMENT

Alison yr 5
St Cecilia's Catholic Primary School Surrey

79

Josh 10
. I would give toys and games for
children that dont have much.

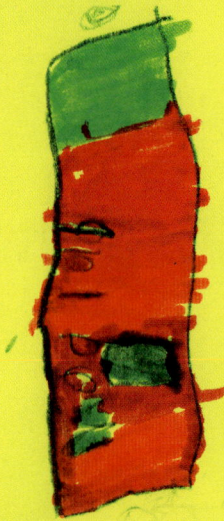

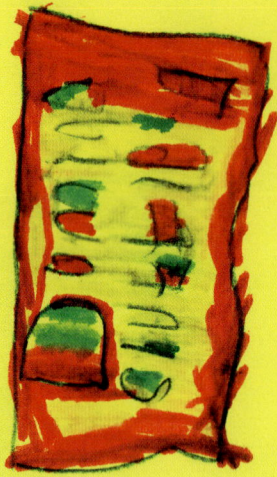

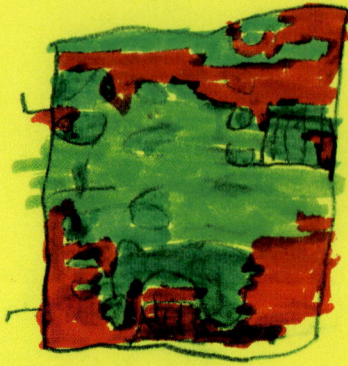

Joshua Cromie
Fleming Fulton School
Belfast

Joshua Cromie aged 10
Fleming Fulton School Belfast

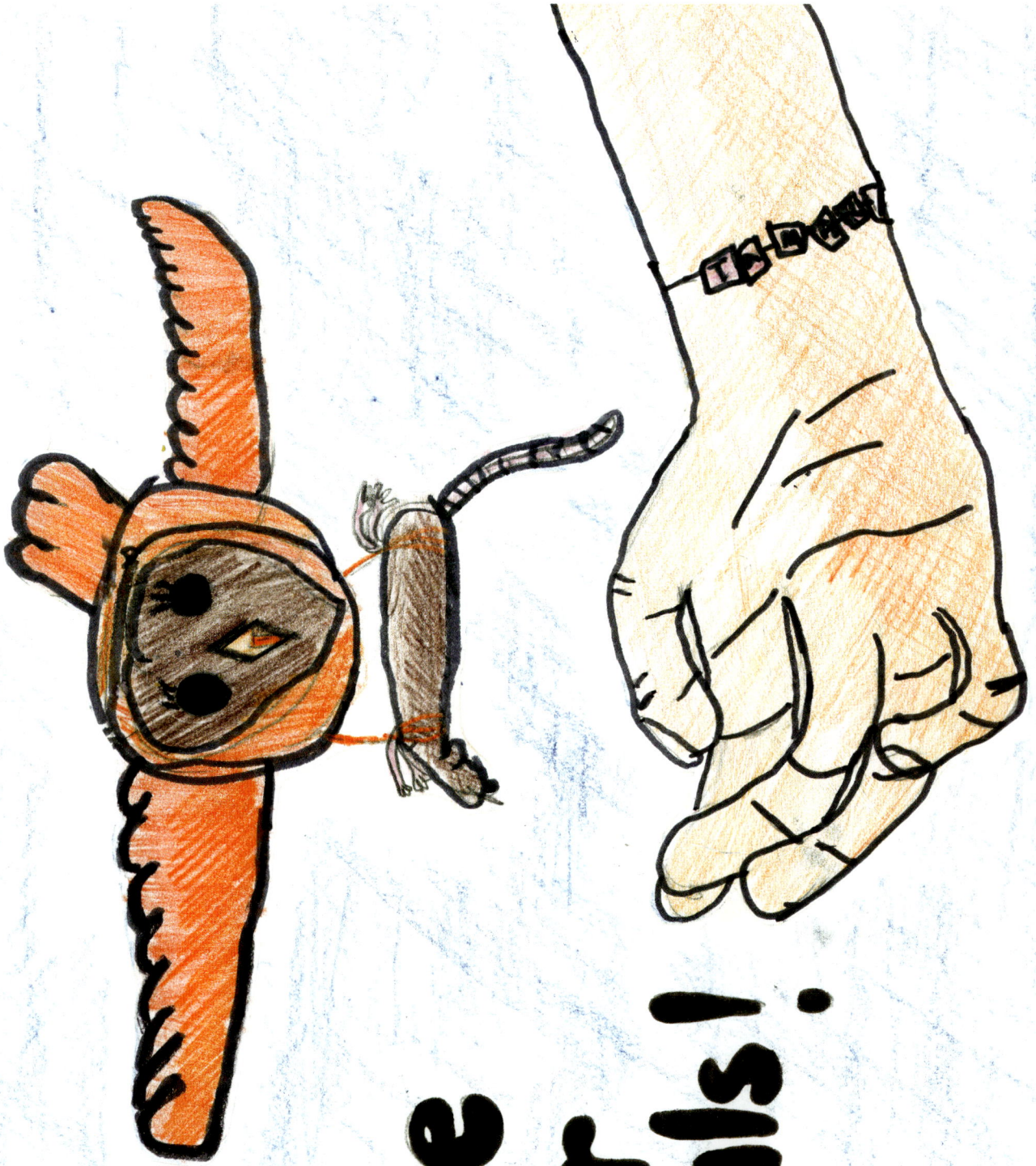

Save our animals!

Tamara Coy aged 9
Canmore Primary School Dunfermline

81

!MY WORLD!

In the future what can I see,
I would like to see it pollution free.
The rubbish, the litter all left lying around,
everyone should pick it up and help turn this world around.
The land fill is struggling, what will we do,
help figure it out, cause it does affect you.
Recycling is the future for me, let's join together and make our
world FREE!

I would like to see our world kept clean,
that means free from pollution, make everything green.
Think of our lives and how we live,
what we can change and what we can give.
To make the air all nice and clean,
get rid of the petrol oh... we can dream....

Please improve the world we live in!

!CHILD ABUSE!

One last thing that is close to my heart,
I'm eleven years old and have learnt,
from the start. I come from a loving
home, so I've never felt in a position
where I'm alone.
I smile to myself when I think
what I have, but then feel for
the children I know might be
sad. I read it in the paper and
hear it on the news.
It really makes me angry to
hear a child abused.
I watch the ads on the telly and I
feel for that child,
let's put a stop to child abuse,
Please make their lives
WORTH WHILE!!

!HOMELESS!

I love my friend I love my foe,
Why should a person not have a home.
I have been to places and seen some faces,
A man I saw once, all tattered and torn,
He had a box, a paper.... I scorn.
I think more should be done, to help people like this
as life is for living, so PLEASE let's start GIVING.
If things don't change, the number will soar,
if I had my way I would OPEN MY DOOR!!

!EDUCATION!

Education Education is where we must start
train the brain, to help us go far.
Employ more teachers, encourage learning
Unemployment, homeless and poverty will be
the turning.
The future of our generation revolves
around our EDUCATION!

!FIGHTING!

My world would be a better place,
if the fighting stopped and we became one
race.
So many loved ones go to war,
the young, the brave, the father in fact all.
They risk their lives to fight for what,
the Government, the country they live
in soon forgot.
If all the Government sat and talked
I would tell them it should be PEACE not WAR!

!ELDERLY!

There comes a day when we are born
We get looked after kept nice and warm.
The years soon pass and we get old, it would be nice not to be left in the cold.
If I could change one thing for the elderly it would be to make sure they are looked after
tenderly. We come into this world needing support so why not when we get old are we not given anything!

Name: Shannon Christie   Age: 11 Years ...

Shannon Christie aged 11
St Margaret of Scotland Catholic Junior School Luton

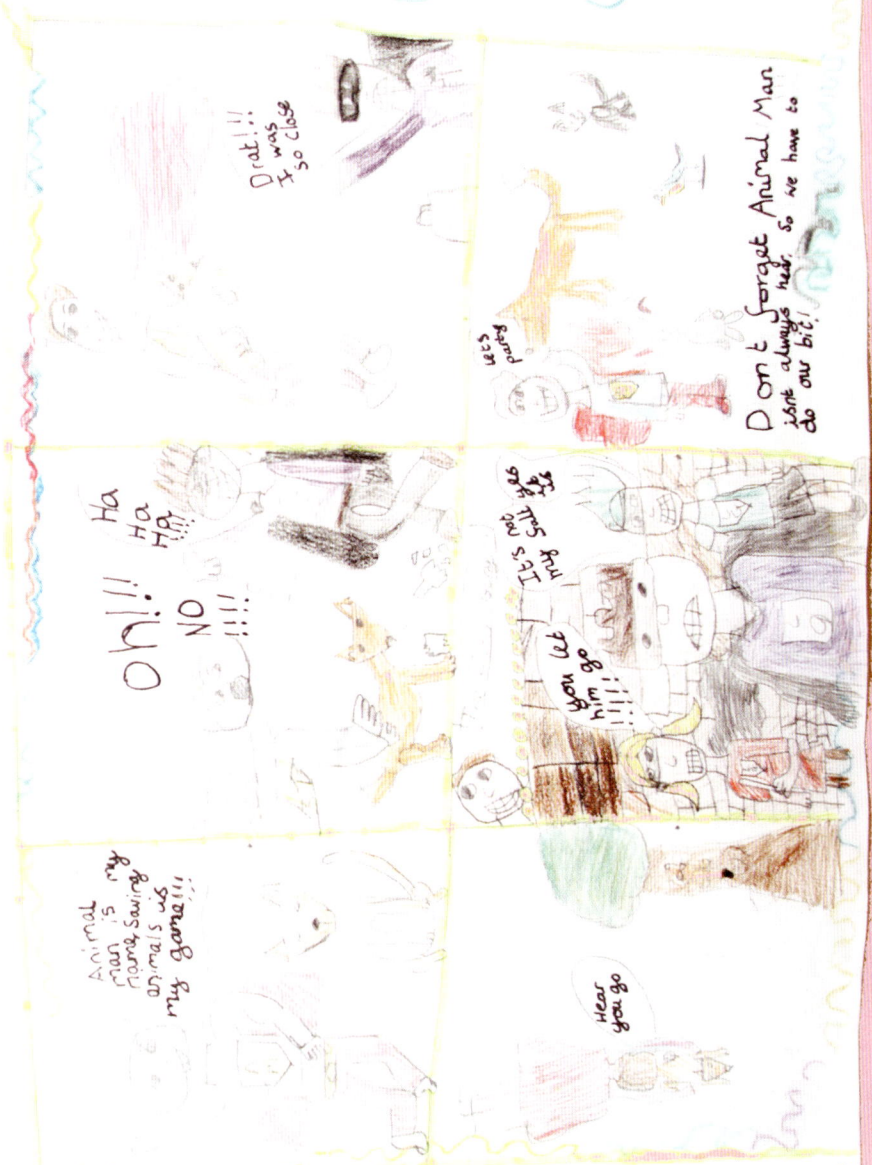

Chloe Saunders, Alice Millard, Nuala-Beth McKeown, Rhianna Mills aged 9 & 10
Budbrooke School Warwick

Class 6 Daniel. Doroodvash aged 11
West twyford Primary School
London Borough of ealing

Have more houses So more people can Have nice houses.

We really need help for our endangered animals.

Recycle Save trees the help us live.

Stop the gun crime here.

Have a wonderfull Clean enviromont e.p graffti.

We need S.O.S fast

"How would we improve the world....."

We need all your HELP!

First you have to get throw us!

We are trying use water carefully "but we need more"

WE Need a Hero!

Stop wars

We can try to give more money fo charities.

N

What is the point!

So YOU Must

Set a good example.

graffti

Daniel Doroodvash aged 11
West Twyford Primary School London

REDUcE ReUSE BICYclE

Don't waste
Electricity and don't
water.

P L A N E T

2. plant more trees.
Protect wild - life

Save

Our

Shannon O Kane
St Brigid's Primary School N Ireland

85

POVERTY

MAKE POVERTY HISTORY

This is an african hut. It was made out of leaves and dirt.

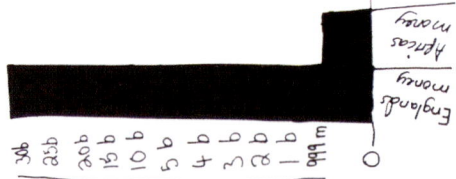

They need more medicine.

In some parts they need more food and water.

My friend Peter has been to Africa and he saw how bad it was. He told me that it was absolutely horrible.

30b
25b
20b
15b
10b
5b
4b
3b
2b
1b
999m
0

England's money   Africas money

Kieran Lowley, Peter Taylor
Goodrich CE (VC) Primary School Ross on Wye

How would we improve the world we we in.....

No pollution

No litter

NO CRIME

Have more Houses
So people have a

Have no gun
CRIME
RIP

Have more
jobs and
Business

Sebri Addows, aged 11
West Twyford Primary School
London Borough of Ealing

N

Sebri Addows aged 11
West Twyford Primary School London

87

Don't Poach!

Joe Woodward, William Skelley, Jamie Donnelly aged 9 & 10
Budbrooke School Warwick

POVERTY

I'm Sanjay and I'm sad because I had hardly any food, I have torn clothes, an unstable house and I live on my own clothes and I live on my own because my parents died of a terrible disease called malaria.

Now that the government has given a bit of money to my country, I now have amazing food, new comfortable clothes and a stable house which is perfect for me and my family.

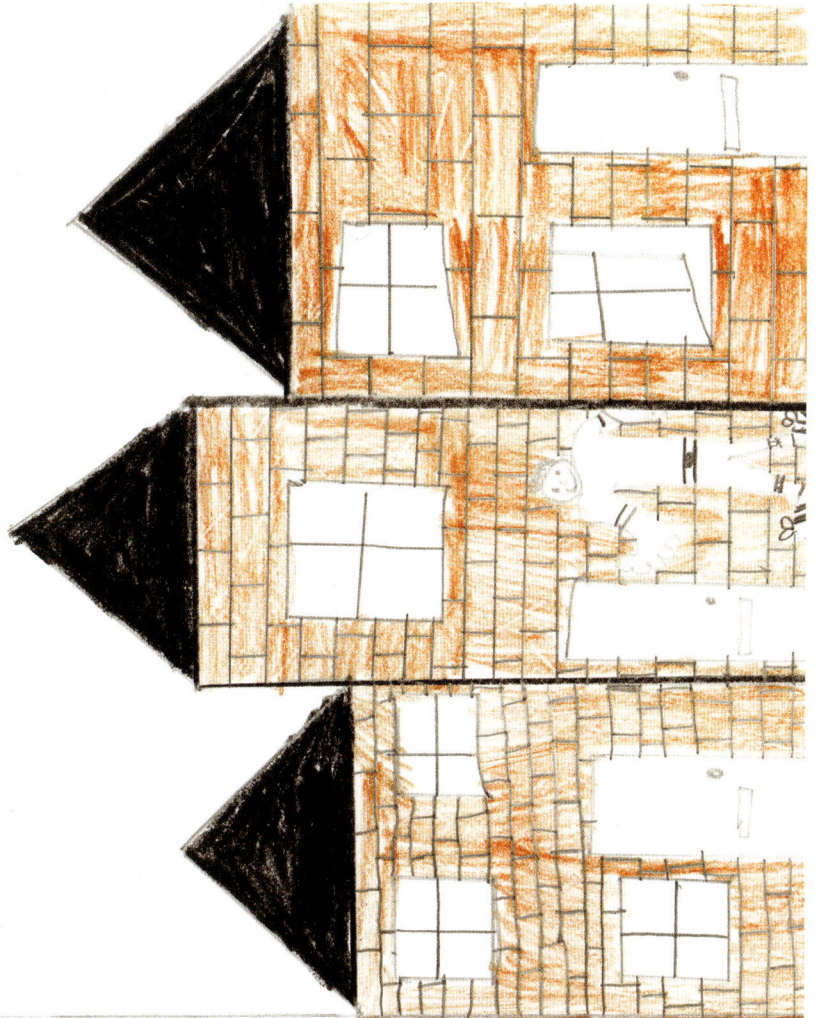

Jake Appleton, Tom Horgan aged 10
Longwick C of E Combined School Bucks

To change the world!

· be Polite

· turn the tap off while brushing your teeth.

· Have happy People

· no cruelty to people and children

littering

I think it would be great to change the world by...

· ban smoking and all drugs that cannot help you in any way and stop making them;

· pick up dog poo and bin it

· no fighting

· sell more healthy food not more fatty. Think healthy!

To help global warming much! To help global warming cars so not using

· no cruelty to Animals

Alison Pilton aged 10
Castle Primary School Somerset

Please Recycle

Please recycle! When you recycle you somtimes have a choise of where to put your rubbish like glass, paper, wood and plastic and lots more, so please remeber to put your rubbish in the most sensible and the most suitable place. Thank-you!

Bottles	Cans	Paper	Glass	Card	Clothes	Plastic	Food

These are some of the things we recycle.

Please Please Please Recycle!

Hannah Scothern aged 9
Coates Lane Primary School Lancashire

RUN

CYCLE

WALK

JOG

Walk or run!
(Driving's not
fun!)

Cycle or jog
you could walk
your dog.

YEAR 6

BY Aleesha Ehoda

Aleesha Ehoda Yr 6
Braunston C.E. School Daventry

Damaging

Stop Environment!!

Stop throwing litter on the floor Put more in the bin to keep the Environment Saye.

STOP

Stop Graffiti because it makes the Environment look ugly and scary.

Stop Graffiti

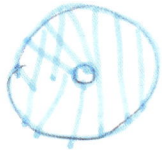

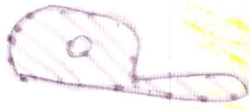

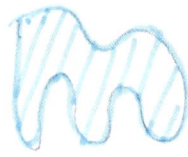

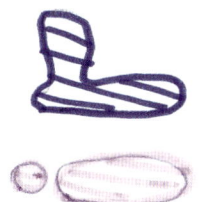

Sehar Hamid aged 10
Hawthorns Junior School Lancashire

Dylan Dickinson
St Aidan's Catholic Primary School Merseyside

Plant more trees!

Fewer trees cut down!

by Hattie Lewington class 5

Hattie Lewington Yr 5
Braunston C.E. School Daventry

I would LiKe people to have enough food and somewhere safe to live

Liam Toland J3/4

Liam Toland aged 10
Limegrove School Limavady

From the question "How would you improve the world we live in?" I decided to focus on my doorstep. Therefore I would like to increase the quality of my local environment – the banks of the river Thames. Some ways of doing this is to: reduce pollution, keep our surroundings in good conditions and not to destroy animal habitats.

Fish
Did you know that we have at least 34 different types of fish that live in the river Thames? Wouldn't it be so upsetting to see them go?

Birds
Here in the region we have a wide range of birds, this is how we can help them: building nesting boxed and NOT cutting down their homes.

Invertebrates
There are many invertebrates in this country and throughout the world. Here are some examples: crabs, worms, bees, ladybirds, frogs, dragonflies and snails.

We can help by:
building nesting boxes – to make it easier for the mother birds to lay their eggs.
creating wooden baulks – so little creatures don't get washed or blown away.
constructing 'brown roofs' where birds can build their nests and where many insects live.
also by keeping all habitats clean by banning non-biodegradable litter.

Isn't nature beautiful? Isn't it important for everyone to live? That's why we need to act NOW!!!!!!!!

And also....IF OUR ENVIRONMENT IS HEALTHY WE ARE HEALTHY!!!!

Thea Ringelstein,
Collis Primary School, Middlesex

Save the World

People don't care, they aren't aware
that the world that we live in soon won't be there
They aren't aware
there will be nothing there
if we don't stop polluting the air
people need cars
to get around
but they don't need gas guzzlers
or very fast cars
all they need is to get around
so get off your butt and walk round
there will be too much water to survive
so jump in and take a dive.

Dylan Alexander McDonald Russell,
Thornwood Primary School, Glasgow

A Better Place!

Stop wars we need peace,

Stop dropping litter and just
put it in the bin it's not a sin,

If you save nature you can save
a simple creature, don't cut
down trees
you can save the bees,

You can help the world and make
it a better place and we will always
have a happy face!

Sarah McBride, aged 9,
St John's Primary School, Barrhead

Stop

I am ten years old and I am growing up
Eleven in May
but I don't count on it.
There may not be a next year.
Just think about it-
We are polluting badly
So stop what you are doing. Think –
The forest where I ride, all trees are gone.
Stop destroying my world.

Beverly Voller, aged 10,
Lavant House School, West Sussex

Loss

War and peace,
Two brothers,
Neither can ever hope to truly win,
Always loss will prevail…

Fate is a cruel mistress.
Sometimes she gives
Certain lands power,
But nothing lives forever.

Death isn't wrong.
Its natural.
But it's when man challenges god himself.
And turns whole countries into desolate waste lands
It's wrong.
So wrong….

When did we lose our faith?
When did our love for this magical world disappear?
That is something only we can answer.

In the end we realize that the battle is far from won,
That we must safeguard life and peace,
Look after this planet that man has made his own
Yet has shamelessly destroyed,
It's not fate that's killing the world.
It's us.

*" I wrote this poem because I wanted to write a really powerful poem about the impact
of war on mankind. Everyone should work for world peace."*

Zak Thomas-Akoo, aged 11,
Rodborough Primary School, Stroud

G
O
O
F
D
a
u

B
r
o
w
n

Graffity is illigel

Graffity because of Graffity

racism is not allowed

Don't smoke Because you can die.

a lot of drugs is madth for you health

never be racist

the Economy of

Obey the rule of

we should keep the world tidy

Graffity is wrong to

Haveesa Kaneez aged 10
Hawthorns Junior School Lancashire

I would change the world by stopping climate change. I would make people cycle or walk to places and only use cars when needed. Stop people flying to so many destinations and make them take holidays in their own country. Everyone should recycle more – paper, glass, plastic bottles. Send unwanted clothes and shoes to charity, so less clothes need making. Encourage people to save electricity by turning their TV's off stand-by. Here is a rap of how you could improve the world.

Climate change just isn't cool
Recycle paper that's the rule
Climate change isn't cool
Turn those lights off – don't be a fool!

Come on guys don't make me frown
Go on - turn that radiator right down
Polar bears need that ice
Come on people lets be nice!

Have a shower not a bath
Climate change is not a laugh
So take that T.V. off stand-by
Come on guys don't make me cry!

Save the earth and its atmosphere
Don't let the rain forest disappear
Come on kids lets save those apes
We've got to do what ever it takes!

Oliver McCaffery, aged 10,
The Grange Junior School, Cheshire

Environment

Litter, Litter everywhere,
On the ground and in the air,
Skies are grey with dirty black smoke,
Let's just think our world will choke,
Pollution, pollution is so not cool,
Just wise up you silly fool,
Little birds in the air,
The fish are choking in the river down there,
The equator is shrinking day by day,
Let the world have its say,
No more drop lets just stop.

Tyler Black,
Hart Memorial Primary School, N Ireland

My Ideal World

My Ideal World is harmless
It's full with laughter and joy

We keep the air clean
Not polluted as if its mean

My Ideal World is green
It's full with tall trees

My Ideal World is glamorous
Because it's full with smiley faces

I wish my Ideal World wasn't just an Ideal World!

Ryhima Jadoon, aged 10,
Hawthornes Junior School, Lancashire

Destroyers

People destroying,
Destroying the world,

Bombs a BANGING,
Tanks a CLANGING,
Wolves a RUNNING
Gunners a GUNNING

Why?
Because of humans
Destroying the world.

What if there was no man?

No bombs a banging,
No tanks a clanging,
No gunners a gunning,
Wolves a howling,
Bears a growling,
Owls a hooting,
We can't get rid of man,
But we can change the future,
We can start to care,
We can work for peace.

Jed Palmer, aged 11,
Rodborough Primary School, Stroud

The Rules for Everyone

Yo yo its Blair
Don't pollute it's not fair.
At the football do not fight
I mean come on that's not right.
Go on your bike, don't go in a car
You could end up as an eco star.
Don't smoke, it's a joke.
Too much drink should make you think.
Everywhere I look there is litter
It's making me feel kinda bitter
Don't kill wildlife they have rights too.
I'm trying to save the Planet
What about you?

Blair Hughes, aged 10,
St John's Primary School, Barrhead

POVERTY POEM

All around the world
Children dying (every 3.6 seconds)
Parents crying
Governments lying
What have we got to do?

All around the world
In the west
We've got the best
Food, clothing and all the rest
Who have we got to help?

We've got to:
Send our socks,
Clothes and frocks
Donations from our money box
That's what we've got to do

All around the world
Make governments donate
Get food on the plate
The poor can't wait
That's what we're going to do

This is what we're going to do:
Allow everyone to live
Get governments to give
If we all pull together as one team
We'll make the world a better place.

Dear Mr G Brown
Every 3.6 seconds a child dies of disease!!! Just think whilst you are reading this letter and poem, about 20 people have died already!!! Imagine how many people die every year (around 65,000). we as a country have to send donations to poor people all round the world. If we all work together then the world can be a better and fairer place.
Yours faithfully
Victoria Jessop

Victoria Emma-Louise Jessop, aged 9,
St Sebastian's C of E Primary School,
Berkshire

I am your home!

The world is like one big home it's full of
people we love and know
It's not all so good in this big home it's full
of the sick and poor and so much more
I wish, I wish the world to be pollution free

The trees are where the rubbish is
dumped but the trees are everywhere
I wish the place we call home was clean
and happier to live in

All I want is the world to talk to tell us
what's wrong and what's making it sad
If the world could talk I bet it would say if
I am not dead I soon will be

So pick up your act or get out of this
place
Save me now or let me die because I am
your home and this is my poem

Megan Young, aged 10,
Thornwood Primary School, Glasgow

The Magic Box

I will put in my box

A sign of precious love and happiness
Astonishing sign of friend ship
The light of thunder and lightning

I will put in the box
A sparkle from the first shooting stars
The clear blue sky

I will put in the box

My loving family especially my brothers!!
Colourful present from Christmas day.

My box is made from
 Lilac silk covered in the snow

I shall surf on my box on the mountain of
Scotland and bambar castle

Clare Kelly, aged 10,
Moorfield Primary School, Cheshire

The magic box

I will put in the box,

A shooting star from the first millennium,
Mystical words from a wise, old wizard,
Magical speech from a fairytale book.

I will put in the box

The first three words of a smiling baby,
Clear blue waves from the Atlantic ocean
Crystal white gems from a cloud

I will put in the box

A eyelash from the fairest princess
The most delicate feather from the whitest dove
The loving tears of a woman's eye

My box is fashioned with lakes as blue
as the sky and stars glinting in the dark sky
And ruby's as red as blood

Laura Taylor, aged 10,
Moorfield Primary School, Cheshire

Education for all

More time to talk to people who can help.

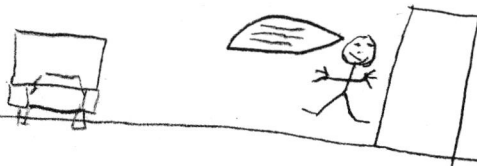

More breakfast clubs in school.

Andrew Moore
Limegrove School   Age 15.

THIS IS HOW I WOULD IMPROVE THE WORLD I LIVE IN….
MY SONG….

THINK ABOUT IT

V1
Do you wake up every morning
And hear there has been a murder
Over here..and..there..
Why don't you ban
Everyone from buying knives and guns
Unless they have a license and show it
Like the soldiers, OH YEAH!!!

CHORUS
Think about it?
Think about it?
Think about it?
Stop the stabbing and the shooting
Just give this world some peace.
Never kill the animals
Let them have their peace.
Don't cut down the trees it's bad
Use both sides of the sheet.
Stop the pollution it's not good
Just cycle or walk to all of the places.
Get the poor some food
They've had a hard enough life.
THINK ABOUT IT!

V2
Why do you kill the animals it's so cruel
Just for a handbag or a very woolly coat
How do you think they feel with no wool or skin?
Leave them alone
Give them a break
Just think about it?

CHORUS

V3
Why cut down the trees
It is also the animal's homes
Just for paper why
Would you all used both sides of the sheet please
It's better for you and
The animals think about it?

CHORUS

V4
Stop the pollution it's not good
Keep care of the environment
Don't drive to close places
Just simply walk or cycle
It's so easy
So just think about it?

CHORUS

V5
We all should simply give stuff to the poor
Like food and water
They don't get much of that
I'm sure they'll like it
It would probably change their life
So please just think about it?

CHORUS

Joel John Armstrong,
Hart Memorial Primary School, N Ireland

My list of rules on how I could improve the world!!

No more <u>bullying</u> or hurting other peoples feelings
Give food, money and clothes to poor families.
Don't destroy other people's property.
Don't vandalise parks! We kids get very cross!
Treat others how you would like to be treated.
Don't be a litter bug, pick rubbish up and put it in the bin.
Spend time with friends and family. Never fall out with anybody.
Don't build too many houses in the countryside. It will destroy the landscape.
Look after elderly people. Checking up on them could save a life.
They will enjoy the company.
My last and most important point is, always listen to what children have to say.
We deserve to be heard!

Michelle McMullan, P5,
St Brigid's Primary School, N Ireland

War

Bombs exploding
Tears of fear
Drip onto the bloodstained streets

Buildings crumbling
Homes destroyed
Families broken
Into pieces

Lives are lost
Over nothing
The dumbest arguments
Many are destroyed

We must end this
Never ending nightmare
Bring together a world
Of peace and love

We will replace
Fear with joy
We will replace
Death with life

" I want to grow up in a world
where there is no weapons, no war
and no fear."

Jack Cullimore, aged 11,
Rodborough Primary School, Stroud

The Magic box

I will put in the box
the first steps from a baby,
the last wrestling match from the Rock,
And the last kick of the game by Jonny
Wilkinson.

I will put in the box
the whitest snowflake of a winter's day,
the tick-tock of a grandfather clock
And the last six from Brian Lara.

I will put in the box
the largest wave of the wild Atlantic,
the greatest fin from a great white shark,
And the cutest baby panda.

My box is fashioned from sparkling stars
and the edges are made from a
fairy's sprinkle of magic dust.

I shall treasure my box always,
I shall look after my box
and play with it everyday.

Daniel Richardson, aged 11,
Moorfield Primary School, Cheshire

STOP THE GUNS

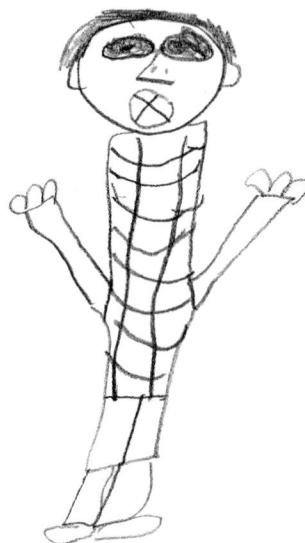

Ellis McGlynn
St Aidan's Catholic Primary School Merseyside

106

Rona's Story

Waves crashed and the storm raged around Sula Sgeir, a tiny island off the North Atlantic coast of Britain, a large bleak rock at the best of times. Many wished the storm would let up, but nature always goes its own way.

A small, white baby seal was sheltering behind a rock. Her name was Rona, named for another island near by. She shivered, and peered out from her hiding place. It was virtually impossible to see anything; the spray blown off the top of the huge waves got in her eyes. She cried out for her mother three times – but no reply. Again, Rona called for her mother, but again, nothing. Rona curled up, while the sea lashed viciously against the rocky shore. Then, out of the corner of her eye, she saw something – not the sea, or the storm, but a huge bird.

The bird was an albatross although Rona did not know this. His head was as white as Rona's fur but his folded wings looked almost black as the night sky. He strutted across the rocks but was not looking in Rona's direction.

"Help!" Rona cried, praying that the bird would hear her. Looking round, to where the voice was
coming from, he saw nothing but a rock. "Good heavens!" he mused, astounded. "A talking rock!"

"No, I'm *behind* the rock!" shouted Rona. The bird peered behind the rock and saw the beautiful seal pup.

"Oh! Sorry, I didn't see you there. What are you doing there?"

"I'm Rona – I've lost my Ma, and no matter how loud I call, she won't come back."

"Well, your Ma can't come back until the storm has calmed. If she tries to come onto the beach in this weather, she might get smashed onto the rocks. The oceans can be very dangerous you know. I am Albert the albatross, by the way."

"I am pleased to meet you" said Rona nervously. "I've never seen a bird like you before – are you special?"

Albert sighed. "I come from the Southern ocean and shouldn't really be up here. I got caught up by an immense storm some years ago and got swept up here away from all of my friends and family."

Rona felt sad for her new friend but did not know what she could say to make him feel less lonely. Then she thought that if she could take his mind off his loneliness, it might make him feel better. "Will you tell me about your life here, Albert? It would make me feel so much better to listen to a story."

Albert looked into the seal pup's pleading eyes and his heart melted. As he began to talk, in her mind's eye Rona saw huge expanses of open ocean. She went soaring over the cliffs on distant shores, and plunging into the sea in head-long dives to catch fish.

"Oh, it all sounds so wonderful! I wish I could soar and glide like you, Albert."

"But you will – just not in the air. You will learn to soar and glide in the water when you are a little older you know." Albert replied. "But it isn't all wonderful – there are dangers everywhere."

"Do you mean things like this storm?" asked Rona.

"No, we animals learn to cope with the danger of the natural world. I am talking about the dangers that humans create – they pour foul tasting liquids into the seas, they throw all kinds of rubbish over the sides of their ships. The strange thing is, they also take fish from the water and eat them."

"But aren't they afraid of being poisoned or hurt by eating fish from dirty water?" Rona said.

"I don't know," said Albert thoughtfully, "it puzzles me a lot. All I know is, little one, if the water tastes strange, you should fly, or swim away quickly. It will make you sick and might even kill you. I once saw some gannets get covered in some black stuff that came out of a human ship. They could not fly, and when they tried to clean themselves, it made them throw up and they got more and more sick until they died."

"Don't the humans care?" asked Rona. "Why do they let such things happen?"

Albert looked at her sad little face. "The way I see it, little one, there are two kinds of humans. There are the ones who care and the ones who don't care. The humans who do care protect some places like Sula Sgeir and stop the bad things being put into the water. We need many more of this kind of human – that way all of the oceans can be clean and safe for all of us."

Suddenly Rona noticed that the storm was dying down. As the wind began to drop and the waves settled down, Rona saw he mum swimming towards her.

"Ma!" shouted Rona.

As she got to the shore, the mother seal saw Albert, and said, "Oh, Albert, thank you for looking after her!"

"It was my pleasure!" Albert replied, winking at Rona. "And remember what I've told you, Rona – it may be a long time before I see you again, I roam over many hundreds of miles of ocean and may not be back here for several seasons. Good luck with the soaring and gliding when you are grown. Goodbye my dear, goodbye."

"Bye, Albert!" cried Rona, and watched as Albert climbed up onto the top of the rocks and unfolded his huge wings. Soon Rona saw him gliding up and up into the rapidly clearing sky towards the rising sun.

"You know, Ma," Rona said, "I think that Albert has a message for all of us. Maybe someone should try to tell the humans to take better care of nature!"

THE END

n.b. Albert the albatross is a real bird who has been spotted at various bird colonies around the Scottish coast since 1967. Originally from the South Atlantic, he is likely to remain alone for the rest of his natural lifespan of 70 years.

Hope Warner, aged 10,
Highclare School, Birmingham

ECO-OUTLOOK
Tuesday 25 September 2027
£1.00

Whales are Back!

Blue Whales – thought to be extinct

A pod of blue whales has been seen in the South Atlantic after 18 years of frantic panic after experts claimed that the animals were classified as extinct.

The Chairman of the Whale Institution, James Foster, said "This is marvelous news. Now we can start increasing the whale population"

Slough gets a new Wetland Centre

People were amazed today as the new Slough Wetland Centre opened for business. The site was previously one of the country's largest land-fill sites. Work started in 2010.

Slough's Land-fill site

Cool Earth

Since the invention of an emission free fuel 10 years ago, the planet has started to cool down. Yesterday, scientists announced that they have found evidence of the ice- caps returning to their original size.

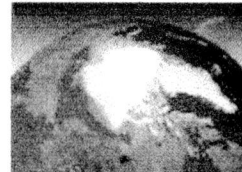

The Polar Ice Cap

Oxfam are heroes!

Oxfam has announced that after 20 years of battling against poverty and starvation in Africa, that they have won the battle against wide-spread starvation, thanks to millions of pounds being raised by fun days across the World.

If we change our ways, this could be what we read in the newspapers in 20 years time. If we don't…

William Lister
Collis Primary School Middlesex

Our Father,

Who art in Heaven,

Help us to make,

A greener and better world,

Where people protect,

The beauty that you have created,

By not dropping litter,

And let us not use,

Plastic bags

But lead us to recycle,

But deliver us from laziness,

And let us use public transport,

For thine is the beautiful kingdom,

The planet and the Universe,

For ever and ever,

Amen

Olivia Tenquist, aged 11,
 The Grange Junior School, Cheshire

How would I improve the world?

If only I could be given
the power to improve the way
children were treated.
I would make sure that
every child had the right to
live in a secure house.
Every child would have the right to
have a loving family,
Loving parents who would care for them.
All children whatever their colour
need a loving home too,
just like me,
Throughout the world,
everyone should have
the same rights as me,
to live safely,
drink clean water
eat fresh food
and live a good, safe life.

Hannah Mogford, aged 9,
Clun Primary, Neath

The Magic Box

I will put in the box.

Words from the song American idiot.
My heart and my soul.
The feathers of a dove.

I will put in the box.

A leaf of a Hawaiian palm tree.
My jet black fluffy puppy.
A single feather of the whitest dove.

I will put in the box.

The sun on a hot summer day.
A snowman with a bright orange nose
A curly pink pigs tail.

My box is made from the finest silk and the
Jewels of a rich man.
I shall fly to the moon and land of the million
craters with my box.

By Calum Whitmarsh, aged 9, Moorfield Primary
School, Cheshire

LITTER

Litter litter everywhere
They throw it down
They just don't care.
You will be fined
ONE HUNDRED POUND!
If you drop it on the ground.
So pick it up
Put it in the bin
To improve the world
We all live in.

IMPROVE THE WORLD

I would improve the world I live in by getting everyone to recycle reduce and reuse their rubbish.

Lots of things can be recycled like – clothes weeds and plastic bottles.

To do this every house should get a recycling bin an ordinary bin and a compost bin.

I would put bigger and more colourful posters around the town so everyone can see them.

We can have special bins to put all around the town.

There are symbols on packaging that tell you to recycle or not – we should make the symbols bigger.

Fine people lots of money - £100 if they drop litter on the ground.

Have talking cameras telling people to pick up their rubbish and recycle it.

When we get our groceries we should reuse the plastic bags and reuse some of the packaging and bottles we buy.

Everyone uses a lot of petrol electric gas and coal and eventually it will all run done. Its much more healthier to walk than take the car. We should try to holiday at home more often rather than taking a plane. Turn your lights off when you go out of a room.

If everyone recycled reduced and reused things our fuel would last much longer and there would be much less waste of materials. This would help to improve the world.

Amy Cheeseman,
Hart Memorial Primary School, N Ireland

Act Now

Where have they gone?
What will they do?
Just think of the last tiger,
Locked up in a zoo.

What's happened to the fish?
They're no longer there,
Pollution has taken its toll,
Leaving the ocean bare.

Why can't we do something?
Before it's too late.
NOW IS THE TIME.
Not two thousand and WAIT!

We HAVE to do something,
Nature needs our aid.
We WANT the earth the way it was,
WHY DO YOU THINK IT WAS MADE?

"I wrote this poem because I am very
concerned about animals becoming
extinct and how cruel people like
poachers can be to them."

Alf Lear, aged 11,
 Rodborough Primary School, Stroud

Save Our World

Don't litter and more recycle
And don't leave the tap on
Do not leave the light on
Don not abduct anyone
Or no abuse to anyone
Or even killing anybody
Try to get on more buses than cars
Don't do firework, animal cruelty
Don't cause any fights
Don't sell anybody guns
Only the police or the good army people
Don't record in the cinemas or get pirate
copies
Try not to swear
You should have more binmen.

Sean Forde, aged 10,
Thornwood Primary School, Glasgow

One of the Ways to Save the World

Save all the trees,
So you can save all the bees,
Keep the plants and flowers,
Get disable ramps don't be cowards,
Donate money,
Don't eat sweets eat more honey,
Get more education for more than one
child,
Some peoples' education is still only mild,
Clean out rivers, lochs and ponds,
As you help you will become eco James
Bond's
Let the homeless have their say,
Then we'll all have a brighter day.

Gillian Crisp, aged 10,
St John's Primary School, Barrhead

The Sky is blue
The grass is green
No-one is My World is ever mean

Wars are ended
Power is clean
There's food for all, what a wonderful
scene

The towns are tidy
The roads are clear
The singing of the birds is all I can hear

The people are smiling
And talking like friends
Lets hope this dream never ends

This doesn't have to be a dream
This really could come true
Who could make this happen?
The answer…. Me and You!

Anna Williams, aged 10,
The Grange Junior School, Cheshire

Friends Forever

relation

improve 4 Friends

enjoy having Friends

No fighting or breakup

do a thing that make smile

Thats all for yous

Sophia Shaikh aged 11
Hawthorns Junior School Lancashire

Krystian Maksymiak aged 9
St Margaret of Scotland Catholic Junior School Luton

RECYCLE

AND OUR SAVE WORLD!

! Recycle TO make our Planet Greener!

Recicle
Cans Paper

! Don't bin stuff that can be recycled !

Amy Orr
St George's School for Girls Edinburgh

116

STAND take out the evil take out the menace DO
up getout and get active and play tennis NOT BE
to ban those evil horrible drugs SCARED
BULLIES keep them weapons away from thugs
get the police out lookin' around
don't let gangs throw litter on the ground
try not to get ya dogs get vicious
because the police are gonna be suspicious

make sure you know the number 999
'cause its the most important phone line
don't take action if you're goin' through hell
or if you do you'll end up in a prison cell
stand up
For what
is right everie bous stand
alone
by Sean Kelly

MAKE IT RIGHT

Sean Kelly
St Aidan's Catholic Primary School Merseyside

STOP GUN CRIME

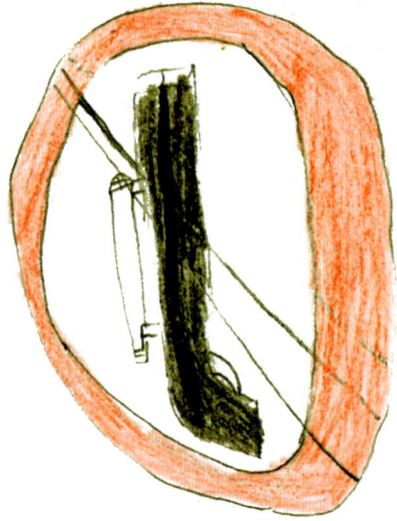

Saif Bashir aged 10
Hawthorns Junior School Lancashire

118

I would like to donate clothes to poor people because it is important for them to have clothes. Ashleigh Lendrum

Ashleigh Lendrum aged 10
Fleming Fulton School Belfast

Lets paint our **DON'T** Rub it out World today! Tomorrow!

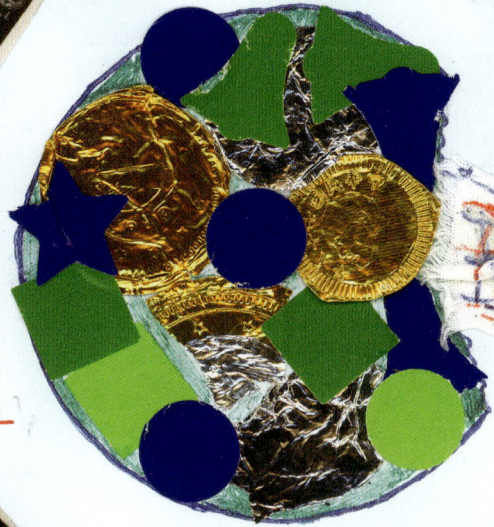

pollution

Waste of water.

Switch it off when you are not using it.

Recycle your rubbish.

Cycle or walk.

Giovanna Scozzari aged 10
St Cecilia's Catholic Primary School Surrey

Toxic Waste

Cut down on toxic was recycle plastic, paper or otherwise it will be poisonous waste.

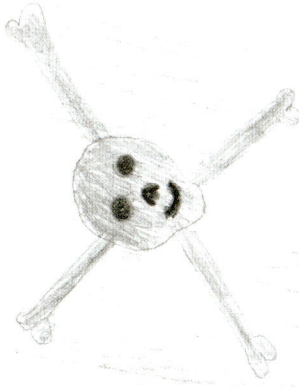

Energy Saving

Start to use more energy Saving light bulbs. Don't put your T.V on standby.

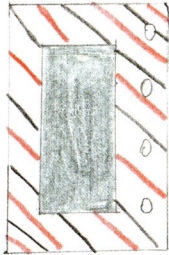

Recycling

Cut down on the waste and use recycling bins. Recycle paper, plastic and many other things.

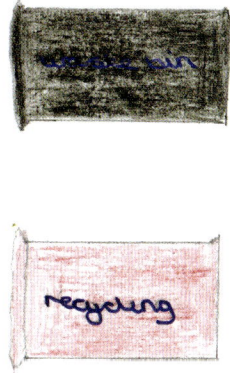

Make a Cleaner Environment

Make a cleaner environment. Don't litter, put your rubbish in the bin and make the world a better place.

Don't use as Many Cars

Use more buses, it can hold more people and get a family share one car.

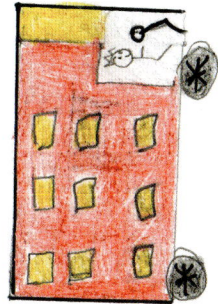

Pollution

Don't use your car as much and on School days do light shares. Don't dump waste every-where.

Libby Swan age 10

Libby Swan aged 10
Lavant House Chichester

In Finland You can sell your bottles and the buyer recycles them.

Margrete Urquhart
St George's School for Girls Edinburgh

PLASTIC GLASS PAPER COMPOST WOOD CHIPPING

Rain water collection

Catherin McMullan
St Brigid's Primary School N Ireland

123

Paris Johnson aged 10
Lavant House Chichester

124

I would like to take away
the rain so we can play outside

Niamh Quinn aged 10
Fleming Fulton School Belfast

Hannah Clarke, Zaylie Ormsty, Bethany Kapma, Grace Cain aged 9 & 10
Budbrooke School Warwick

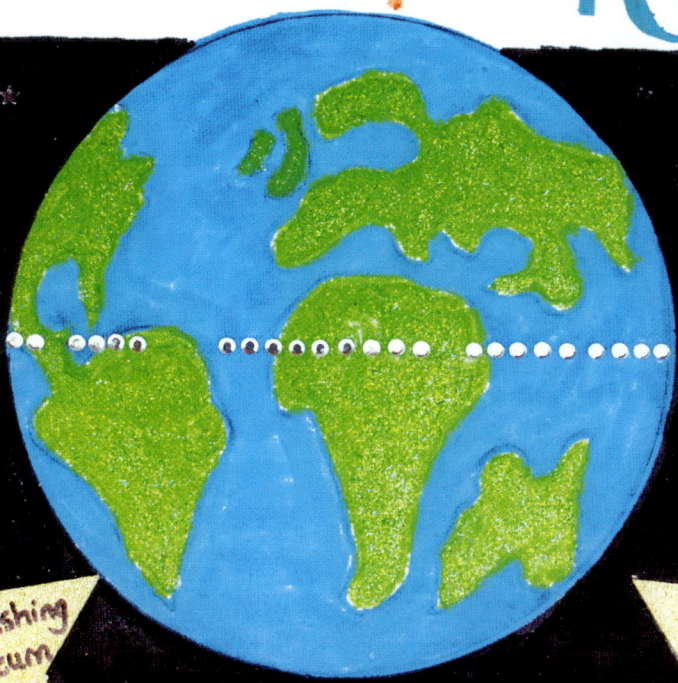

Lauren Martin
St Brigid's Primary School N Ireland

127

Improving the World

I would improve the world by not throwing cans into the ocean, because dolphins and other fish in the sea could drink a bit of a fizzy drink, and it could poison them!

Also if you go fishing use a fishing rod not a net because dolphins can get caught in them!

Think of the Sea Animals

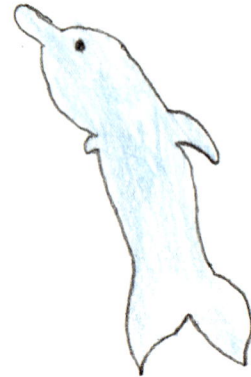

Recycling is going to help by stopping global warming, so put your cans and things in a recycling bin.

By Hannah Cargill (9)

Hannah Cargill aged 9
Lavant House Chichester

STOP!

Cars grumble wearily
Pouring out poisonous steam
People stumble unable to breathe
As the world cries out in pain

STOP POLLUTION!

The beautiful rolling countryside
Now buried under bricks and mortar
Crawling slowly, like a nasty virus, houses and more houses!
Where has the wildlife gone?

STOP THE COUNTRYSIDE DYING!

They keep on laughing
Like they're having a fit
Pointing their finger at the little girl
She runs away desperate for a loving family

STOP RACISM!

There she sits an English girl
With a banquet of every food imaginable
While a poor African girl is
Feeding her brothers whatever scraps she can find

STOP POVERTY!

Screaming gunfire shatters the air
The sound of war echoes across the land
The sharp cold cough
Could be his last

STOP WAR!

STOP POLLUTION
STOP THE COUNTRYSIDE DYING
STOP RACISM
STOP POVERTY
STOP WAR
FULL STOP

"I wrote this poem because I wanted to express how I feel about the world today and what we need to change."

Olivia Hinkley, year 6, Rodborough Primary School, Stroud

Together

We must all live together in harmony
Together we must take responsibility
To make our world a happy place
Where everyone can live in peace in their own space.

Where there is war and starvation
We must work together for peace
There is so much food to share
It is up to us all to show we care.

Guns and knives make us all unsafe
The streets round our homes feel like a scary place
The laws of our land must be respected; we are all affected
We must stand together to wipe out violence forever.

We live on this planet for such a short time
From generation to generation we pass it down
The Earth is our home and we must respect it
Litter and pollution really affect it, it is up to us to protect it.

Every small action is worthwhile
United we can change our world one step at a time
Across all continents we must come together
To make our world a better place forever.

Stephanie Semple, Collis Primary School, Middlesex

How would I improve the world in my life

I think people who are poor
should have money.
Every child should have a mum and dad
to hug,
to make them food,
to help them with their work and
most of all be there for them
when they're lonely or sad.
I would make people recycle more
Stop them from smoking,
Protect their environment.
People need to stop chopping down trees
and think about the homes of the animals
that they are destroying
People need to look after the world better
People should respect our world.

Morgan Jenkins, aged 9,
Clun Primary School, Neath

I DREAM OF...

I dream of a world with no wars
Where everyone safely closes their doors,
Peace and kindness for all of us
Stop making such a fuss.

Graffiti should not be on my wall
Because it costs too much for us all,
Spray paint damages the Ozone layer
While people try to sort out who's the
Mayor.

We should stop polluting the air
Because it is really unfair,
Public transport is far the best
Use your feet, give engines a rest.

Craig Ferguson, aged 9,
Canmore Primary, Dunfermline

How I would improve the world we live in...

How we can stop the polluted world from forming:

Share cars when we need to or all the time
Recycle clothes and old rubbish
Cut down on the amount of telly we watch
Don't put your playstation on standby, save your game and turn it off
Put cycle sheds in your school and cycle to school – it keeps you healthy
and saves our planet

Save our planet!

Olivia Frances, aged 9,
Braunston CE Primary School, Daventry

Change the world to make it a better place!

No smoking because it has a drug in it.
Walk to school and stop using cars, buses, airplanes, trains, boats.
More helping like cooking school meals.
Do not leave the TV on when you're not watching it.
Turn the tap off after brushing your teeth.
Recycle your rubbish.
Happy people.
If you use both sides of your paper you save trees.
Reduce what you can.
Clean up your dog droppings.
Save the animals in danger.

Jasmine Gosney, aged 10,
Castle Primary School, Somerset

If I could change the world

If I could change the world I would
not let anyone go without food or water.
Everyone would be friends
There would be no badness in the world.
We would all be different
but not be jealous of each other.
If I could change the world
I would make sweets good for you
and make pop run from the tap.
We would never be ill or sick.
We would all get along
like one big happy family.
If only I could change the World.

Rachel Thomas, aged 10, Clun Primary School, Neath

Make this world better
NOW

If i could make this world better,
These are the things I would do,
Id make the animals better to get them out there zoo,
Id stop all the wars for what is the cause,
Of all this calamity,
We must clean up the city,
But to help stop pollution,
Id need a solution,

But what on earth would it be?
Ahh I know and here it is,
All turn to 30 itll be a wizz,
And sensors to tell a hoax call apart,
So when a service is needed they can dart,
To the pepole who really need it,

So why cant we see,
What destroyers are we?
What wound have we given are poor world?
It is like we are curled,
Up in a habit we cant escape,
My are we toatally ape?
We need to change this world right now,
And this.........is..........how.

Global warmings my biggest fear,
When I heard about it I shed a tear.

Megan Singleton aged 10
Castle Primary School Somerset

Recycle your waste don't put in bins
There's paper and plastic, glass and tins
Keep to recycling its easy alright
Think about the world a much better sight

Now let's move onto packaging we all use too much
Use plastic bags, boxes, baskets and such
Take your own bags, buy local veg
Compost it later – it's great for your hedge

Use your cars less walk if you can
There are buses and lorries there's cars and vans
Walking everyday is so much healthier for you
You can walk, jog, run even bike to!

So I hope my poem has made you think
Keep your eyes open and don't take a blink
Our world is changing rapidly each day
If we don't change it now it'll go the wrong way

Caroline Glenn, 6L,
The Grange Junior School, Cheshire

Stop wars.

I am like Iraq all angry, ready to attack the enemy, our great britain, going to get a fright when Iraq attacks them right. Of course it might be the other way around, the united kingdom might attack Iraq of course I don't know because the government won't tell me enough. I just wish that the Prime Minister will just cancel the war with Iraq of course the wars just like a game. Someone has to lose.

Jack Knox Mackie, aged 10,
Thornwood Primary School, Glasgow

How to Save the World

The world is like a bouncy ball
Throw it down it'll bounce back up

Why use it as a weapon?
Why use free people to start a killing spree?
When they could be free like me?

and Why eat a jelly bean when you
could have a Green Bean?
Why let people get away with racism?
We're all the same.

Why can't we be just like me?
and why pollute the ocean?
Why are drug dealers not the Headline?

I KNOW!

Let's stop and mop up this old cold world
Why not keep some jelly beans but grow more green beans
Let's stop and get to the top with drug dealing
Let's make guns banned or pour them into the bin!

Now that's how to save THE WORLD!

Rob MacKinnon, aged 9, Thornwood Primary School, Glasgow

My Perfect World

My world would be a beautiful place
where everyone would have a smile upon
their face

No battles or wars to be won
my world would be full of fun

At one with brothers and sisters together
We can ride the storms through all kinds of
weather

No religion or need
can alter our creed
we will do this together
forever!

Shannon Ferguson, aged 9,
St Cecilia's Catholic Primary School, Surrey

How I would improve the world I live in

I would stop
all wars taking place in my world
because wars destroy
countries, towns and villages.
War brings orphans, terror, bloodshed.
Loved ones will be lost forever.
People would lose their homes
and possessions.
Most of all their lives.
Lives are precious
Lives cannot be replaced
In my world I would like
Peace.

David Ridge, aged 10,
Clun Primary School, Neath

Ugly,
Eiffel Tower look-a-like,
Zzzzzz Bzzzzz Szzzzz
Annoying bee sound-a-like,
DANGEROUS
Waste of beautiful space.
PYLONS

Amazing,
Beautiful flower look-a-like,
Brrrrr Wrrrrr Brrrrr
Whispers **in the air**
USEFUL
Protector- a shining white angel.
WIND TURBINES

We composed music to perform our poem.

By the boys of Year 5 and Year 6 Hurworth House School

A pendulum poem to sing......

Shade		Protect
Oxygen		Breathe
Art		Beauty
	Trees	

Food		Energy
Home		Shelter
Life		Tomorrow
	Trees	

Our Earth

Our tomorrow

By the boys of Year 5 and Year 6

Hurworth House School

135

Killing Animals

Some people think that right is wrong
When it comes to killing animals
Like the elephant for its tusks and feet
How would you like it if they killed you?

Some people think that right is wrong
When it comes to killing animals
Like the rhino for its mighty horn
How would you like it if they killed you?

Some people think that right is wrong
When it comes to killing animals
Like the honey badger for its teeth
How would you like it if they killed you?

Some people think that right is wrong
When it comes to killing animals
Like the knarwhale for its twisted tusk
How would you like it if they killed you?

Some people think that right is wrong
When it comes to killing animals
Like the crocodile for its tough skin
How would you like it if they killed you?

"I feel very strongly about all the greedy
people who kill animals for unnecessary
reasons."

Raoul Hodgson, year 6,
Rodborough Primary School, Stroud

Our World

Our world is a wonderful place,
So don't make it a disgrace,
So stop littering now.

STOP pollution now,
Walk, bus or go by train,
Even in the rain.

Start saving energy,
Turn off your lights,
And the world will be healthy and bright.

Hannah Moriarty, aged 9,
St Cecilia's Catholic School, Surrey

A song called:

THE ENVIRONMENT CAN CHANGE!

Chorus

The environment can change,
if we all do this together,
the world will be a better place,
for everyone one one one ohh!
(hold for 3 seconds)

1-2-3-4

Chorus

If we recycle,
yeah recycle, yeah recycle (hold)
the world will be more clean,
Ohhh Clean (hold)

5-6-7-8

Chorus

Now for litter,
yeah litter, yeah litter (hold)
the world will be more clean
Ohhh Clean (hold)

9-10-11-12

Chorus

What about pollution,
yeah pollution, yeah pollution (hold)
and if stopped,
we could breath clean air (hold)

13-14-15-16

Chorus

17-18-19-20

Sofia Maria Boyall, aged 9,
St Margaret of Scotland Catholic Junior
School, Luton

How I would improve the world live in

Africa, India, countries like that
Should have some more clean water,
And every single parent
Should appreciate their son and daughter.

You effect the environment
When you smoke,
You also harm yourself
Because you can choke.

All people should get along
Black and the white,
And every single person
Should have their own rights.

Amber Slavin aged 9
Clun Primary Neath

Cleaning up the World.

The UK produces around 330 million tonnes of waste each year, a quarter of which is from households and business. The rest comes from construction and demolition, sewage sludge, farm waste and waste from mines. Our throw-away culture is risking people's health and stealing the world's natural resources. Making so much new things, uses up the world's valuable natural resources.

Waste disposal companies collect waste from waste producers and take it to waste disposal site. The most common types are landfills sites but other methods include re-cycling plants, incinerators and composting. Most of the things that end up in incinerators and landfill can be used again. Landfill sites are the most used method of waste disposal. The gas generated during decay can be used to generate electricity. This however can be a waste of useful resources and can also produce liquid and gas that can be harmful.

Recycling and investing in waste reduction would go a long way to solving the problem. Instead the Government prefers burning it at incineration plants, like the one planned for Cheshire. About 10% of England's waste is incinerated.

Part of the solution is composting, it removes the need for landfill or incineration. It saves natural resources and reduces greenhouse gas emissions. However, planning permission for composting sites can be difficult, as they are unpopular with local communities. But any energy that is recovered from natural wastes can be regarded as renewable energy. It comes from plant material, animal wastes, paper or card. This then can also be used to replace fossil fuels instead of being left to decompose naturally; it could help to limit the emission of carbon into the air.

This will help against Global climate change which is the single biggest environmental threat facing the planet!

Adam Cunningham, aged 10,
The Grange Junior School, Cheshire

Save the Earth

Save the nature, it's in grave danger
If you give to the unfortunate you will be affectionate
Please put your litter in a bin, if you don't it is a sin.
Stop the war and all this fighting, it doesn't do us any good
Stop the global warming if you want lighting
Try your best at school, you'll be very cool
Save the planet, you'll be a hero
When you smoke it is not a joke.
This is what I want for the world.

Megan McLean, aged 9,
St John's Primary, Barrhead

WATER

BEFORE I FINISH THIS POEM
LOTS OF CHILDREN WILL DIE
'COZ THEY HAVEN'T GOT
FRESH WATER
SHOULDN'T THEY HAVE A
SUPPLY?

WOULDN'T IT BE
BETTER?
WOULDN'T IT BE
FAIR?
IF WE SORTED
OUT FRESH
WATER,
TO SHOW THAT
WE CARE?

IF ALL THE WORLD WAS
EQUAL,
IT WOULD BE A BETTER
PLACE.
NO MORE CHILDREN
NEED TO DIE,
LETS PUT A SMILE ON
THEIR FACE.

Flora Blake-Parsons
Collis Primary School Middlesex

The Magic box

I will put in the box

Melted chocolate from the finest chocolate bar
A crystal clear icicle from a Christmas tree
And the first word of a new born baby

I will put in the box

My first birthday present from my my mum and dad
The shiniest bolt of lightning in the sky
The first silver tear of my sister.

I will put in my box

The first hug of my sister
The first conker of a tree
A feather floating through the sky

My box is fashions with silk and gold with snow on
the lid and lightning in the corners.

By **Liam McCann**, aged 9,
Moorfield Primary School, Cheshire

Stop Child Abuse!

Im battered and bruised
Im shaking with fear
I just want to know
When he'll be here
I've got marks there
and marks here
Im just a little girl
I want to get out of here

I want to be like my friend
Im really scared I want it
to end
I want to tell someone
I just can't find it in me
Leave me alone
I want to be free.

Jade May, aged 11,
Newlands Primary School,
Southampton

Follow the Peace Rules!

Come on ya'll lets make the world a better place
You have to if you want to save the human race,
Use your bike more often than car
And you'll become an Eco Friendly Star.
Put your litter in the bin
You've just committed one less sin,
Always eat your dinner
Don't become a sinner,
Give to the poor,
Don't flush your brain down the sewer,
Just be cool
Follow the peace rule
Don't be a fool,
Don't smoke
It's just a big joke!

= PEACE =

Chelsea McCann, year 6,
St John's Primary School, Barrhead

HOW CAN I IMPROVE THE WORLD I LIVE IN

I would try to reduce the amount of wasted created by my family by recycling bottles, paper, tin cans, clothes, shoes, toys and plastic. All of those items can be brought to our local recycling area and charity shops where they may be able to be used again by someone else. If we don't reuse all of these things then we are going to keep using the world's fuel and energy in order to keep making these products and this will have an effect on our environment.

I would ask my dad to make a compost heap where we could put vegetable peelings, old fruit and vegetables, grass cuttings, egg shells and egg boxes, hedge cuttings and other food waste. This compost can then be used around the garden in flower beds to help other plants to grow. I would also collect rain water in a barrel and this could be used to water the garden plants and lawn. It is much better to use this type of compost than by using other fertilizers and chemicals.

I think that I could help reduce pollution by walking, cycling or sharing lifts with my friends and family so that one car could take a full load to the BB or other activities instead of a whole lot of cars taking one person each in them. This would reduce the pollution that has an effect on the ozone layer and also means that there are less cars on the road and this means the roads are safer.

If our houses were insulated better then it would take less fuel to heat them and also heat would not escape through the roof or windows. This means that there is less waste of energy and fuel.

I would try not to waste as much food by only cooking enough for the meal and not cooking extra just incase I was hungrier than I thought. Left over food is normally not eaten the next day but put into the bin.

I could also check the dates on food before buying it so that the food would not have to be thrown out before it was able to be used because the sell by date has passed.

These are just a few ideas of how I would improve the world I live in. Everybody should help us do all of these things and maybe we could make a difference to our environment.

Stefan Heyburn,
Hart Memorial Primary School, N Ireland

A Lonely World

Wondering through the lonely forest,
I glanced at an empty tree stump,
I sank onto it quietly,
When I realised what it could be.

The tallest tree for miles around,
Large, great and strong,
Children would play around its trunk,
But now, its chopped right down.

Wondering through the lonely forest,
I glanced at an empty stalk,
I touched its skin quietly,
When I realised what it could be.

Gracefully a petal floated by,
As the great wind sighed,
A child would admire it from above,
But now, no life is seen.

Wandering through the lonely world,
I glanced at an empty clearing,
I stared at it quietly,
When I realised what it could be.

The trees of the great forest once lent over many fields,
With poppies blazing red like the setting sun,
Happiness and joy spread around the earth,
But now everything is fading.

Do we really want this to happen?

"I am concerned about animals and their homes being
destroyed by deforestation. Governments should take
action now!"

Rhianne Baxter, Yr 6, Rodborough Primary School, Stroud

Carl.

 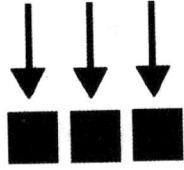  

I want   everyone   in   the   world

to   be   happy.

Carl McVeigh
Fleming Fulton School.

Carl McVeigh aged 10
Fleming Fulton School Belfast

Daryl Saving the World Rap

Come on y'all let's pick up da pace
We can make the world a better place.
Saving the world it's all about dat
If you do this you'll be the top cat.
Please stop smoking I know it's hard
Now come on I know you really want that I'm not a smoker card.
Don't waste money
It isn't very funny
Please come to school it's like a vacation
If you do this you'll get a better education
Okay y'all that's all I have to say
I know you can do it let's have a pollution free day.

Daryl Convery, aged 10,
St John's Primary School, Barrhead

OUR WORLD!!

There's lots of litter on the ground,
Blown, thrown and scattered around.
Why do people leave it there?
Is it because they don't really care?

Put it away into a bin,
Leaving it there is just a sin.
Dispose your rubbish in a sensible way,
Recycle it, reuse it, or throw it away.

Save on water, energy too,
Lets save our planet, it's up to you.
Turn off your tap when brushing teeth,
Turn off your light when going to sleep.

Saving our planet is the right thing to do,
Watch what you do and it will look after you.
Don't take the car when you go to school,
Walking is just totally cool!!!

Emily Carter, aged 9,
St Cecilia's Catholic Primary School, Surrey

The Magic Box

I will put in the box
The rich colour of an olive tree,
A white dove with a silver wing,
The sweet taste of apple pie.

I will put in the box
A drop from the deepest sea,
Along with the joy and laughter from a fair ground,
Tiger woods last put as he raised the club.

I will put in the box
A video game turned bad,
Freddie Flintoff hitting a six whilst
Kaka scores a goal.

My box is fashioned from diamond and jade,
With devil on the corners and spotlights all around.
The hinges are the hands of a baby.

I shall fly on my box
To France, America and maybe even Mexico,
To meet superman and save the world.
It's a wonderful box.

Liam Smith, aged 10,
Moorfield Primary School, Cheshire

Monica   Molina:
     (10)

What can you see in this picture? In this picture I can see a lot of water and a lot of ground but a little forest ... and you know for why? Because a lot of people trow the rubbish to the ground and contaminate the Earth. For us the children, you need to learn something very important: — WE NEED PROTECT THE EARTH !!!

Monica Molina aged 10
Lavant House Chichester

Don't Spit At People

Ban drugs

Use your talent

Show The Red Card

Be A Friend not a Bullies

Give money to hospal to help people get Better

friend 100–0 bullies

SAVE Our World!

MAKE A DIFFERENCE

guns hurt people

Sweet life nice life or fun?

clean up

Megan O'Toole
St Aidan's Catholic Primary School Merseyside

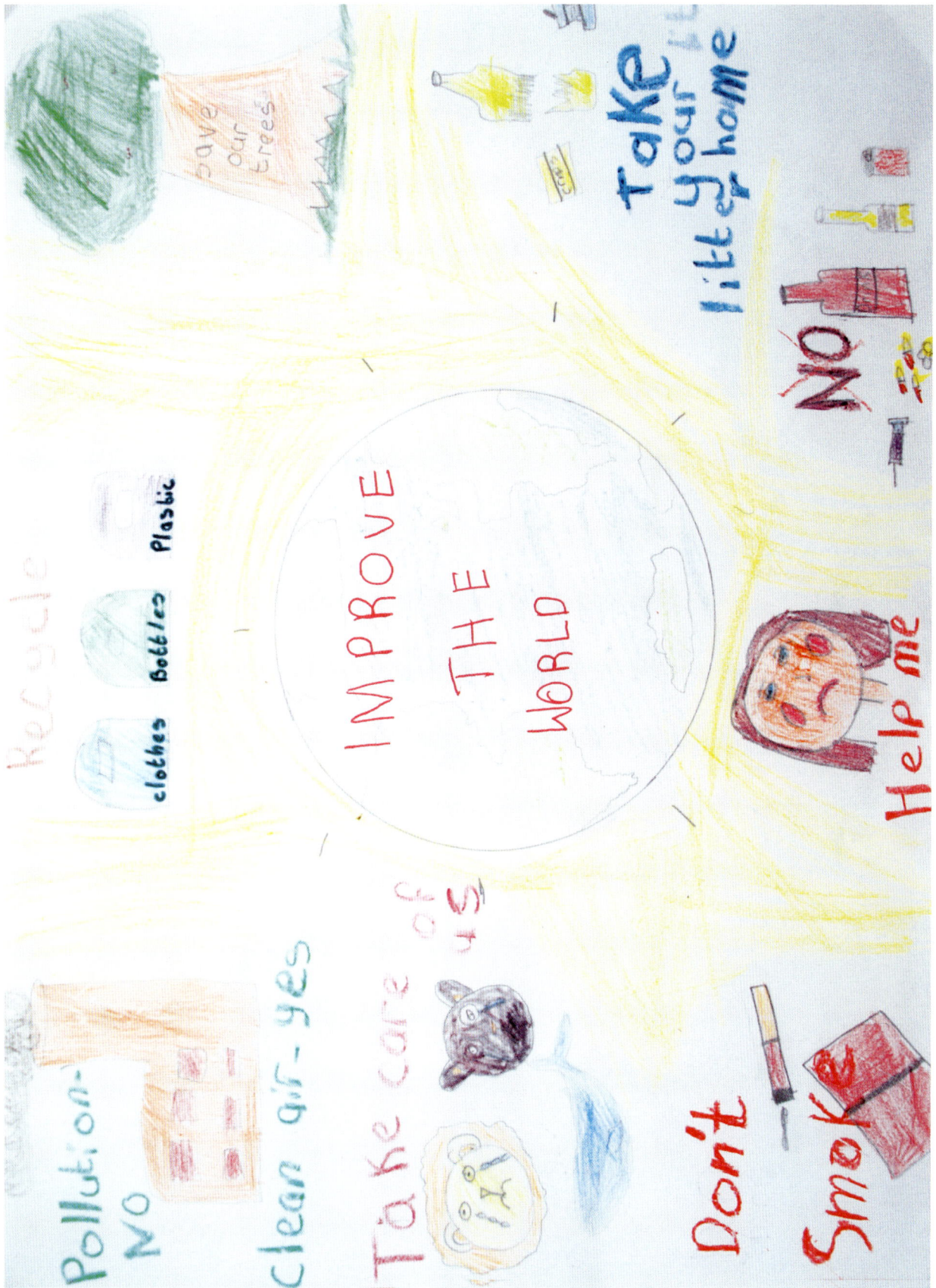

Save our trees

Take your litter home

No

Recycle — clothes Bottles Plastic

IMPROVE THE WORLD

Help me

Pollution — No

Clean air — yes

Take care of us

Don't Smoke

Janet Kelly
St Brigid's Primary School N Ireland

147

How I think we can stop global warming:
- stop global warming:
- get cars of all the
- stop all the manufactoring

Global

WE NEED YOUR **HELP!**

try to contact to countries Heads of the rain forest's that have they can stop and ask if down the cutting trees.

Could you put more recycling bins around town and in school?

WARMING

please stop global warming somehow.......

Stop the ice from melting

ice bags are melting!!!...

RECYCLE

Rachel Chamberlain, Bethan Howe, Daisy Cleeve, Amy Goodman, Elizabeth Rogers
Goodrich CE (VC) Primary School Ross on Wye

Zoe Hopwood
St Aidan's Catholic Primary School Merseyside

Grant Ogilvie aged 9
Canmore Primary School Dunfermline

BULLYING

I BULLYING

ANTI-BULLYING
Stop the bully
it can be changed

STOP BULLYING

ME
miss

Bullying Poem

STOP IT

Turn that frown upside down

Bullying has got to stop and so has child abuse i have to stop it it could change your life and bring a smile to the world

Roxy The bully

Let the sun shine

Lucy Whitehead, Emma Barnsley, Ellie Huxtable aged 9 & 10
Budbrooke School Warwick

151

Ellie Roper, Ellie Lancaster, Phoebe Snow, Millie White
Goodrich CE (VC) Primary School Ross on Wye

NO TO DRUGS AND DRINK THINK! YES TO PUDSY DON'T YOU THINK?

SEND A PARCEL MAKE IT SNAPPY TURN THE POOR CHILD INTO MR HAPPY

LOOK AFTER THE FARMER AND SEE GREENER GRASS AND BIGGER TREE

www.turismodecanarias.com

"HOW WOULD YOU IMPROVE THE WORLD?"

LOOK AROUND MY EARTH AND SEE HOW TO IMPROVE THE WORLD WITH ME

RECYCLE! RECYCLE! RECYCLE YOUR WASTE NO RUBBISH FOR MR HUNGRY TO TASTE

Don't be a litterBug!

DON'T BE A LITTER BUG INSTEAD GIVE ME A BIG FAT HUG

MATTHEW McMULLAN P.5

DON'T POINT A GUN AT ME INSTEAD OF THAT JUST TICKLE ME

Matthew McMullan
St Brigid's Primary School N Ireland

153

More wise

Charity

More hospitals

THE RED Card

Help disabled

4 everd transplodson

Flu cds

more

Stop the bullies

Spitting!

Save our world

Stop cutting down trees

Save our world!

ban knives outside

drouggso

More Food

No Swearing

More water

Smile

No guns

No drugs

Stop egging windows

Try and stop gun crime!

Trees

Food

fight

Steal

bullies

Police

More money

The red card

stop crime

Kayne Forshaw
St Aidan's Catholic Primary School Merseyside

154

My World

GOD Knows

Imagine a world where everyone is alike. No social groups nor poverty, no violence or pollution. That's my dream world. I hope it's true and real.

I wanna live
I wanna live
with no problems in my world
I wanna live
I wanna live
I wanna change my world now 14.15
That's how it should be
that's how it should be

Everytime I walk I see people begging for money I give them a pound or so and wonder 14.15 there I said it. It seems to me if there are two part of a world. 1 where everyone is rich and making fun of others and second one people are poor but still having fun

chorus

Sometimes you see people fight but they never ask themself if fighting is going to solve their problems. you see the snake gang up in the air you may think this is the END!

chorus

NO EVIL IN OUR world

Peace in our world

Helen Nzubi
10½

Helen Nzubi aged 10
St Margaret of Scotland Catholic Junior School Luton

The Environmental Times

29th July 2015

Major countries agree to actions to stop car pollution!

Today the leaders of the largest countries in the world have agreed to make this world a better place by stopping pollution.

The group of countries, that have reached the agreement so far are USA, Russia, Britain and China, but new countries are soon expected to join them.

Pollution has been caused by many different sources, since the last century. Some of the main polluters are car fumes and factory emissions. Fumes consist of carbon monoxide and oxides of nitrogen hydrocarbons.

Vehicle use has steadily increased and pick up trucks, vans and sports cars are replacing cars that are more fuel efficient and give off less fumes.

Part of the problem is that people are thinking that posh and expensive cars make them look rich and successful.

Aeroplanes and boats have been other big polluters recently.

People are wanting to visit places that require huge air miles.

Food is being transported by aeroplanes and boats to our supermarkets when there is enough food to be eaten in our own country.

The leaders of the countries in this new group have decided on some ways to stop pollution getting even worse.

They have decided to:

- Make non polluting cars cheaper to buy and put higher taxes on cars that cause most pollution.
- Design the look of lower polluting cars to be similar enough to the high polluting cars so that people will want to buy them.
- Ration petrol so that needless journeys are not made.
- Making people aware that it is better to walk or use their bicycle.
- Offer money incentives to people who share cars.
- Increase public transport and reduce the cost to use it.
- Reduce the amount of car races.

Hopefully, as more countries join this world wide project, the planet will become a better place to live in.

Report by Joshua Brown

Joshua Brown Yr 5
St Sebastian's C of E Primary School Berks

Child Abuse

Stop people
Killing each-
other!

people dying

you are going to die with him.

Stop people killing each-other!

Stop parents bullying their children!

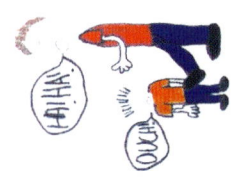

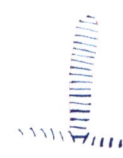

HA HA HA
OWW

Bully the world

Stop the Bullying!

people are getting hurt.

Do you want the world to look like...

...This?

Rules
1. Less smoking
2. more recycling
3. more walking
4. Don't waste food
5. Remember the three r's reduce reuse recycle

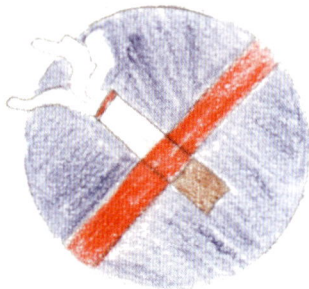

cardboard

recycling

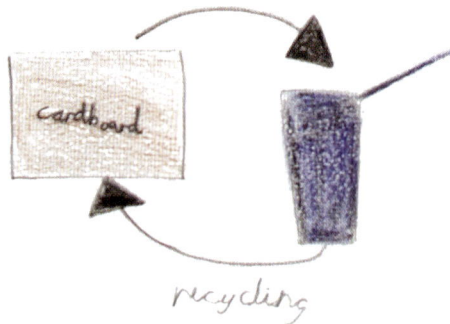

Jude Dillon
St Brigid's Primary School N Ireland

USE IT DON'T LOOSE IT

Take The Road To Recycling

The wrong way Frazzle the Alien is drinking a...

But drops it on the road

The right way Frazzle the Alien is drinking...

But this time Frazzle Puts it in the bin.

In the end Frazzle did the right thing

Well Done 4 Recycling

Recycle

Just Recycling A Plastic Bottle Makes A Big Difference !

3 R'S Reduce Reuse Recycle

Joseph Owen, Jack Beinck

Joseph Owen, Jack Beinck aged 10
Budbrooke School Warwick

Instead of playing with a gun Why don't you just have some fun. In this world don't Be mean, Instead Just be kind of clean. Instead of lighting a very big fire and just don't be a very big liar. Insted of doing the wrong thing and looking like a fool, do the right and Be cool. Instead of destroying a bicycle Just Be good and Recycle.

Ellie Molloy
St Aidan's Catholic Primary School Merseyside

God's Message

God's hand at work
Weaving through the world
Perishing the sparkling litter
Land, land I want to see
Work, work, work!
Brush, broom
Mop, sweep
And whisk it away!
You'll bar the sun,
The moon will weep
And the stars will drift away,
Into the deep, night river.

Punishment is needed!
With the chores I do, I deserve a sweet slumber
In my heavenly cloud bed!
I shall not tell but a sign needs to be gifted.
Green for the sign of the work on the tacky world
And arrows to say I have moved on!
Good luck! Farewell!
Luck will be needed on your charmed challenge
As I watch over you.

Elizabeth Massey, year 6,
Highclare School, Birmingham

To make the world a better place,
you need to look at every face;
different colours, eyes and ages,
Wow! I could write pages and pages.

Respect for cultures far and wide,
understand their need for pride,
people need food and a home of their own,
and someone to love so they're never alone.

I also think that a job and health,
are more important than a fast car and wealth,
but we want to have fun and enjoy the world,
without being scared of terrorists and bombs.

It seems simple to me that we all need to care,
and learn to listen and talk and share,
Politicians are trying their best,
but maybe they need to talk to the rest.

Emily Jones, aged 10,
The Grange Junior School, Cheshire

**How would I improve
the world I live in?**

I would like to stop racism!
What's wrong with black and white?
People are being killed!
It is definitely <u>not</u> right!!

My heart tells me its wrong
no ones strong or weak.
Something has got to be done!
that's exactly what I seek.

Someone's got to change it.
Make the world a better place.
To make everyone happy,
put a smile on everyone's face!

Charlotte Hambly, aged 10,
Clun Primary School, Neath

Save and Improve Our World

Don't take drugs have some tea go to the
shops and buy some new mugs
Stop global warming or when you wake up
in the morning there will be war and we
don't want any war
Save the trees don't fall on your
knee and kill the bugs.
Send the kids to school give
them education and
don't be a fool
help the poor who live in sewers
stop pollution because it is
yucky and could be poison
Don't be a pest - No litter you're
the best!
No vandalism or you might
go to prison! Oh no!

Kerry Friel,
St John's Primary School, Barrhead

<u>YOU</u> NEED TO BE GREEN

Global warming is not new,
It doesn't just affect me; it also affects you.

We have got to stop it now,
And I've got some ideas how.

We could all look really cool,
If we left the car at home and walked to work and school.

If we all stop cutting all the trees down,
The air will be nice and fresh in our town.

If we turn off the lights,
It will let the moon shine in the night.

It would be really fantastic,
If everyone recycled paper and plastic.

To help make the world be clean,
<u>YOU</u> NEED TO BE GREEN.

Holly Pettifor, Year 5,
St Sebastians School, Berks

The magic box

I will put in the box

A stolen kiss
The magical feeling of a heart-warming fairy tale
The seven crystal clear colours of a rainbow

I will put in my box

The first crispy golden leaf to fall of a birch tree
The warm, loving smile of a dear friend
The footprints in the white, fluffy snow

I will put in my box

The reddest ruby eyes have ever seen
The mystical moons reflection on a huge, magnificent lake
The silver sparkle in a mans eyes

My box is fashioned on raindrops, rubys and roses, with hearts on the lid and whispers in the corners
Its hinges are icicles shaking in the cold

I shall perch on my box the pixie dust left behind that has been sweeped away by the wind

Emma Jones, aged 9,
Moorfield Primary School, Cheshire

The Save the World Rap

Hello and welcome to the Save the World Rap,
to start with turn turn off that tap.
Homeless people need somewhere to stay,
all you need to do is give them a pay.
Old toys give them away,
take them to the church this very day.
Put litter in the bin,
and it's one less sin.
Stop wars and fighting it ain't good,
everybody's in a big angry mood.
If you don't listen to these rules,
you won't be really really cool.

PEACE

Nicole Cathcart, aged 9,
St John's Primary School, Barrhead

Show Racism the Red Card

Save our Planet

The world will be a better place
If you help to keep it safe,

Help donate money to the poor so
they don't live in the sewer.

Save the nature you'll be a ranger
because it is in great danger.

Do your best to save the rest,
Send all children to school
You will be very cool.

Save our planet and be a hero
it will be worth it in the end.

Show Racism the Red card

Martin Curren, aged 9,
St John's Primary School, Barrhead

Animal Testing

Why do we allow all these animals to suffer,
We wouldn't do that sort of thing to each other.
For perfume, cosmetics, and shampoo,
Please tell me why we do the things we do.

Every few seconds an animal is dying,
Yet no tears are shed in crying.
We try and convince ourselves that it is right,
Just so that we can sleep soundly at night.

Did you know that thousands of animals die every year,
but, we choose to ignore it and not to hear.
We tell ourselves that this killing cannot be a sin,
Even though innocent lives are just thrown in a bin.

What could they have possible done to deserve this fate,
these animals that trust and show no hate.
Protect my animal's God commanded us,
But we prefer to blindly accept, than make a fuss.

Yet, if we all stood up and worked together,
I know we could stop animal testing forever.
But, we would need to be true and strong,
and accept that what we currently do is wrong.

Thomas Rees,
St Sebastians C of E Primary School, Berks

How Can We Make Our World a Better Place?

How can we make our world a better place?

Do you re-cycle all of your waste?

Do you give money to help the poor?

And do you waste water? Don't do it anymore!

Protect animals and habitats at all costs.

Do you hope litter and pollution will get lost?

Do you turn off lights when you don't need them on?

Be careful or our world will be gone!

Our world is precious, you must take care.

Or else our world will no longer be there.

Class 5RH, Thorne Brooke Primary School, Doncaster

I  would like everyone  in

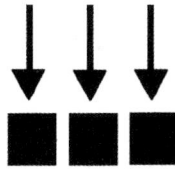

the world to have water.

Megan

Megan McLaughlin aged 15
Limegrove School Limavady

How We Can Change the Planet

Let's start with animal testing
And tell why it's so cruel and unfair
More than 2,567,893 animals are used for experiments
Whether it's pain or not
Don't you think that's cruel and unfair?

Here's a thought we could recycle more
Up to 60% of rubbish in your bin could be recycled
And the largest lake in Britain could be filled with
Rubbish in just eight months
How about we get started now?

What about pollution
Global warming is the worst
Animals are dying out and it's all our fault
So why don't you help the planet by walking to school
Or saving electricity by turning off your light?

These are my ideas of changing
And saving the planet
Do you have any?

"Be the change you want to be in the world"

Naomi Boobbyer, St Sebastian's
C of E Primary School, Berkshire

How could I improve the world I live in?

I would love to see in the world
people hand in hand,
joining together,
Black and white,
Christian and Jews.
Lets be friends together forever.

I would love to see in the world
love and compassion in our hearts,
No wars in this world,
Friends with each other forever and ever.

I would love to see everyone healthy,
Well and together,
No families shot or killed.
No lives lost through war.
People around the world.

Cerys Stanton, aged 10,
Clun Primary School, Neath

Poachers

Poor little animals just want to be free, but watch out theres a poacher about.
Out of the bushes jumps a poacher I think to myself why cant I be free.
All around me there is fear why can't my mum still be here.
Closer and closer they come they're closing in on me.
Hunters, hunters are hidden away if only my friends knew they were still close by.
Early morning Im still awake running from the poachers Im so tired.
Running is too much for me I am getting weaker and weaker with blood trickling all over me.
So now they are gone leaving me a free life again.

Katie Sheath, aged 10, **Hannah Webber**, aged 9,
Newlands Primary School, Southampton

"..*trying to stop this horrible world from poachers.*"

Improving Our World

If you use this car
You will reduce your carbon footprint
Now listen to our hint
Does not need petrol
Does not use oil
Does not have any electric stuff
Does not need the money to run
So...
Forget the money and in with the fun.

Editor's note: *These children drew extensive plans for an eco friendly car, which could not be reproduced in the book. However their ideas included:*

• *Mini wind turbine attached to the electric motors both side*
• *An exhaust pipe that collects cold air and puts it on the engine to cool it down*
• *Lasers on the bottom of the road to make the car slow down*
• *Air vent at front of car as the car goes along a pipe blowing air on the electric motor*
• *Solar panels*

Design features copyright held by:
Scott Gibson, Maddi O'Niell, Henry O'Niell and Naomi Cribson,
Deerhurst & Apperley C of E Primary School, Gloucester

Improving the World

Get on your bike use your feet
exercise you cannot beat.
Leave behind the noisy car a walk to
school is not that far.
Keep the world litter free use the litter
save a tree.
Try to use what's in the bin recycle
recycle don't give in.
Do you really need that light? Are you
watching TV tonight? Is that you PC
shining bright?
Turn off that light, TV or PC remember
you will save energy.
A safe world would be so good.
A world where no ones short of food.
A world where crime is stamped out,
a world where food is shared out.
What I would love to see no guns or
weapons in our society.
No poverty, food for all.

Find a way for us to give take care of the world in which we live.

Robin Graham,
Hart Memorial Primary School, N Ireland

Listen

Cars, trains and aeroplanes
Their fuels turning into gases.
Grining faces turning downwards,
As we look up through the dusty clouds
We see the planets coughing.
We see the moon nodding in disagreement
lost in his own thoughts of angriness.
We have to stop this now
We can't lie in our beds hoping someone
Will do it for us.

Marguerite Parker
St George's School for Girls Edinburgh

Our World

The world has changed in many ways,
Or so I hear my granny say.
So many cars are on the roads,
The winters never seem as cold.

Global warming, I hear them talk
Very few polar bears are left to walk,
I say why don't we try today,
Instead of just listening to what people say.

Take the bus and not the car,
The bus can take you just as far.
Recycle as much rubbish as we can,
Do you really need new pots and pans?

Stop the fighting, killing and drugs on the streets,
Make sure everyone has enough to eat,
Love each other for after all we're all in this world
Together, for one and for all!!!!!!!

Nicholas Topping, year 6,
Hart Memorial Primary School, Belfast

Education Rap!!

You know around the world ya gotta make it fair,
Coz there's children here and children there
And while ya lay back in ya chair
There's children learning nothing there.

I know you know education is rather rare
So you better care.
If other countries start to care education will be
Respected here and there
So come and show us that you care.

Well I'll say goodbye and see ya soon
Spread the word that education must be heard
Frick a frick a work!!!!

MacKenzie Wells, aged 9,
Newlands Primary School, Southampton

Hello Lovely World

(The year 2007 – The Problem Pollution! The solution an 11 year old boy named Ashley Snailham)

There once was a boy named Ashley. He was fed up with the World being polluted, so he promised himself he would make it a better place to live. Ashley wrote a letter to the Prime Minister in Downing Street and the Prime Minister managed to change the world and saved the Earth from pollution and it was all thanks to Ashley.

THE END.

Dear Mr Brown,

I am writing this letter because I am worried about the Earth's health. It is incredibly smelly because of the pollution in the air from the many factories in our country. Please make it better and make our air fresher so we can breathe more and have a better life.

Yours Sincerely,

Ashley Snailham,
ISP Teynham Primary School, Teynham

3 GIVE access to medical treatment

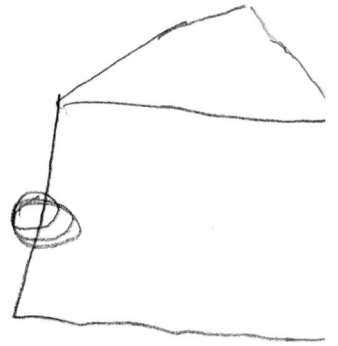

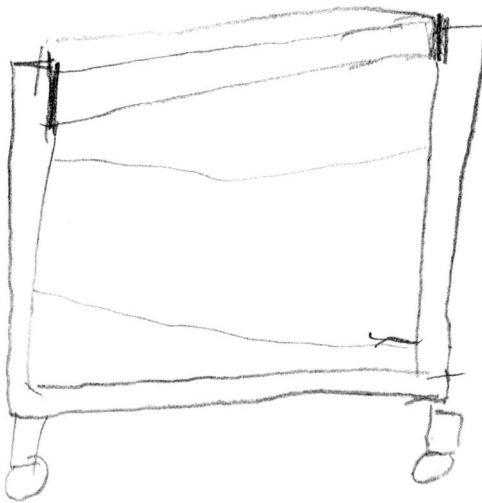

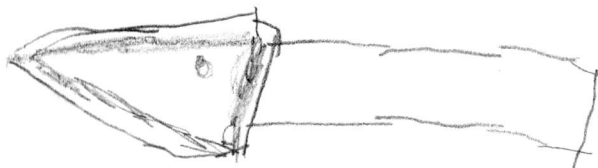

Megan McLaughlin
Limegrove School Age 15.

Megan McLaughlin aged 15
Limegrove School Limavady

Hugh Thomas, Alex Lindon aged 9
Budbrooke School Warwick

8:00 I jump up caring and trying to think, while the world is getting destroyed at the speed of a blink.
As peoples problems turn to a mass mess, all peoples happiness becomes even less.

10:00 I think of the desert and those poor camels with no water, and of course their unfortunate de-hydrated slaughter.
We should share it out, to be fair, so the camels don't evaporate because of us (we do care.)

12:00 Let's start with the ocean and why it's polluted, while all we do is sit-back as if we were muted.
Let's think of all those dying sea-creatures, our heart is thumping, trying to teach us.

2:00 There's lots of fighting and unhappiness everywhere, it's like no-one does actually care.
Why can't we all just be kind? Can't we all be family (at least in our mind).

4:00 What about the Antarctic and the poor polar-bears, while we are melting their ice with our global warming affairs.
Can't we save the ice and be healthier too? If you give them their home back then they will repay you!

6:00 And let's not forget the rain-forest and those trees disappearing. If you stop killing their trees then it's you they will be cheering.
If we can find a way to make our own wood, then they can live in peace like all animals should.

8:00 It's my final say, about how I've improved the world today.
We all may be different, each with a different personality, but if we all came together, we could be one big happy family!!!!!

Olivia Leach,
Collis Primary School, Middlesex

How I would Improve The World I Live in

I would encourage the building of an environmentally friendly car production i.e. battery operated or water powered. In the meantime order a one-day a month car free day which the Chinese have already tried but failed so lets see if making it law would be better.

Electricity is a great drain to our environment. I think it would be good to reduce the price of solar panels and wind turbines so people would be able to buy them more easily. Solar panels use the rays of the sun to heat and power equipment, homes and industrial factories. Wind turbines store energy through the motion of the wind, as both of these are natural production of the planet's own cycle it would be good to utilize them.

Housing and building development is slowly eating away at our agricultural heritage i.e. trees, grasslands, bush and deserts. For every tree that loggers cut down they should by law have to replace twice the amount. These trees once replaced should be allowed to age before being cut down.

Recycling is beneficial but not enough people do it. Industry should be charged if not thought to be reusing properly and world committee should be set up to find any country in the world that could not prove they were recycling accordingly.

For these problems are not one countries problem but the worlds

Matthew Crawford,
Hart Memorial Primary School, Belfast

Timber baulks
Nesting poles
Brown roof

Thea Ringelstein
Collis Primary School Middlesex

How to improve our World

POVERTY

In an ideal world there would be no poverty and no excessively rich people.
The rich would divide their wealth with poorer people.
Everyone should have enough money to provide for their families, feed and
clothe them and be able to provide a warm and safe home.

FAIR-TRADE

Lots of our foods come from poor countries where the workforce are paid a
poor wage and often exploited. Then we end up sending monetary aid to help
them. By Fair-trade it means that the workforce are paid a proper wage and
so they can then support themselves and their families.

BETTER HOSPITALS

Hospitals are getting worst by the second, so we want to improve hospitals by
giving the hospitals a better clean, getting more staff for the patients, the staff
should have better and longer training, and more money invested.

WATER

Water is something that we all take for granted – we turn on the tap and there
it is. Lovely clean water. But what if we had no water/what if we turned on the
tap it was dry? Every living thing needs water to survive.

BUILDING

More and more of our "green space" is being built on and countryside being
destroyed. We need to stop all unnecessary building NOW.

Editor's Note: *This is a small excerpt from a 14 page document the children submitted.
Due to space restrictions, we cannot publish it all. However, the children also covered:
Energy, Pollution, Greenhouse Earth, Renewable Energy, Solar Panels, Windpower,
Wave Power, Pedal Power, Biodiesel, Transport, Grow your own Fuel and Recycling*

Ben Adams, Ben Green, Andrew Torr, Sarah Parker,
Deerhurst & Apperley C of E Primary School, Gloucester

MY GREAT GREEN WORLD

The world I live in is full of wonderful places
So many people with different faces
What a shame it is that people pollute
They kill, they fight and they shoot

From the Arctic to the deserts man has been bad
We have ruined the environment making me sad
The icebergs are melting, so bad for the polar bear
I often ask do we really care

We are using too much gas and oil
At the same time spoiling the soil
The ozone is getting thinner
But I wonder who is the winner?

YOU CAN DECIDE – NATURE OR MAN?

How we can make the world a cleaner place

We can all improve our environment by doing small things in our homes. All these changes added together can make a big difference to reducing our carbon footprint.

Reduce, reuse and recycle
Wind turbines to make electricity
Solar panels to heat houses and water
Wood chip boilers to heat houses
Rain water collection for use in houses
Double glazed windows to conserve heat
Low energy lighting in houses
Composting to use for plants and the soil
Walk to school when possible
Use paper bags instead of plastic bags
Use a bicycle for short journeys

Catherine McMullan,
St Brigid's Primary School, N. Ireland

How to protect our planet

1. I think we should stop cutting down trees because trees give us oxygen. We also need trees for paper, tables, furniture and houses. Remember anything that comes from a tree can be recycled. This would help the world a lot.

2. Try not to take the car to school, just walk because cars and all types of motor vehicles are causing too much pollution and it is really destroying our planet. Remember clean air helps our bodies stay healthy.

3. Using aerosols is not so good either as it is destroying our ozone layer. It is getting thinner and thinner from each person spraying one bit of spray each day. Try to use alternatives such as roll on deodorants.

4. When you go outside or to bed make sure you turn off all light switches and pull out all the plugs out of the socket as it wasting electricity. This will not only cut your electric bill down and saving energy but you will also be helping the planet.

5. In the environment there are lots of boys and girls throwing down litter. It makes everything and everywhere look untidy. Parents will agree with me on this one if there is too much litter then their children play in it and could end up with serious illnesses and diseases, and also it attracts mice and rats.

6. Remember the three 'R's **Reduce Reuse Recycle**. If everyone done a little of this it would improve the worlds a lot.

Planet Earth Poem

Time is running out
Will our planet survive
Pollution is around us
We need to keep the world alive

There is light at the end of the tunnel
There is so much we can do
Reduce Reuse Recycle
You can help too.

Pick up the litter
Turn off the lights
Don't spray that aerosol
And things will be alright

Don't cut down our trees
As we need them to live
Keep the seas nice and clean
You know what I mean

Walk to school
Don't go in a car
Breathe in clean air
And show that you care

There is so much to do
We all need to help
Keep our world nice and clean
'Cause every little bit helps.

Save the world!

Regan McIlveen,
Hart Memorial Primary School, N Ireland

By Megan Webb

I would improve my world by....

Bringing country's togher for peace

And...

Be one with animals

Stop murderous attacks on People.

Stop

Stop World Poverty.

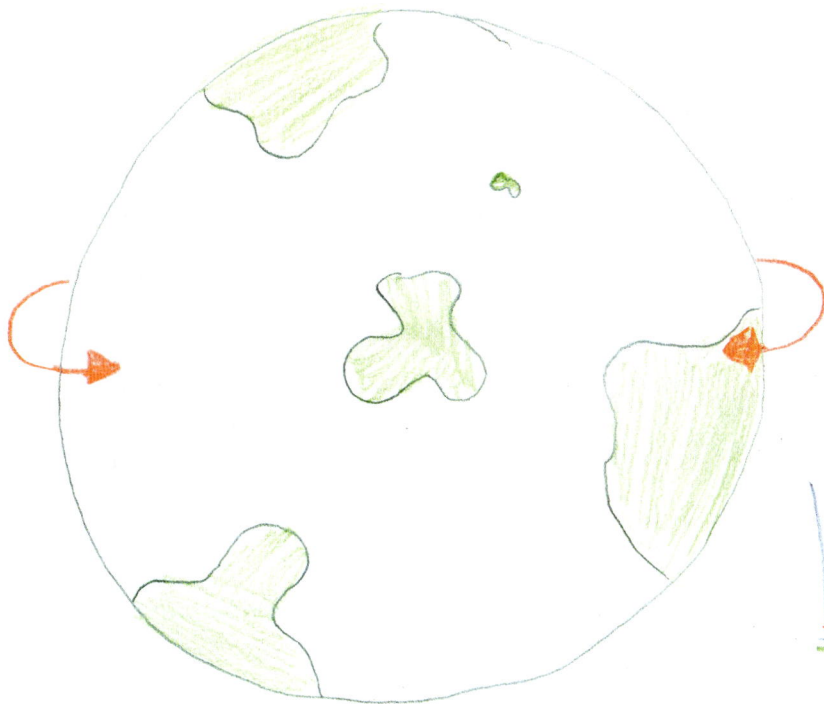

This is how I would improve my....

WORLD

Megan Webb aged 10
Longwick C of E Combined School Bucks

My ideal world

No violence!

Please do not throw rubbish in our rivers!

Put a stop to drug taking and too much alcohol

Please don't pollute our world!

No littering

We need more Police Officers!

No more wars!

Cristina Centracchio aged 9
St Margaret of Scotland Catholic Junior School Luton

LETS CHANGE

OUR WORLD

Georgia Davies aged 9
Braunston C.E. School Daventry

179

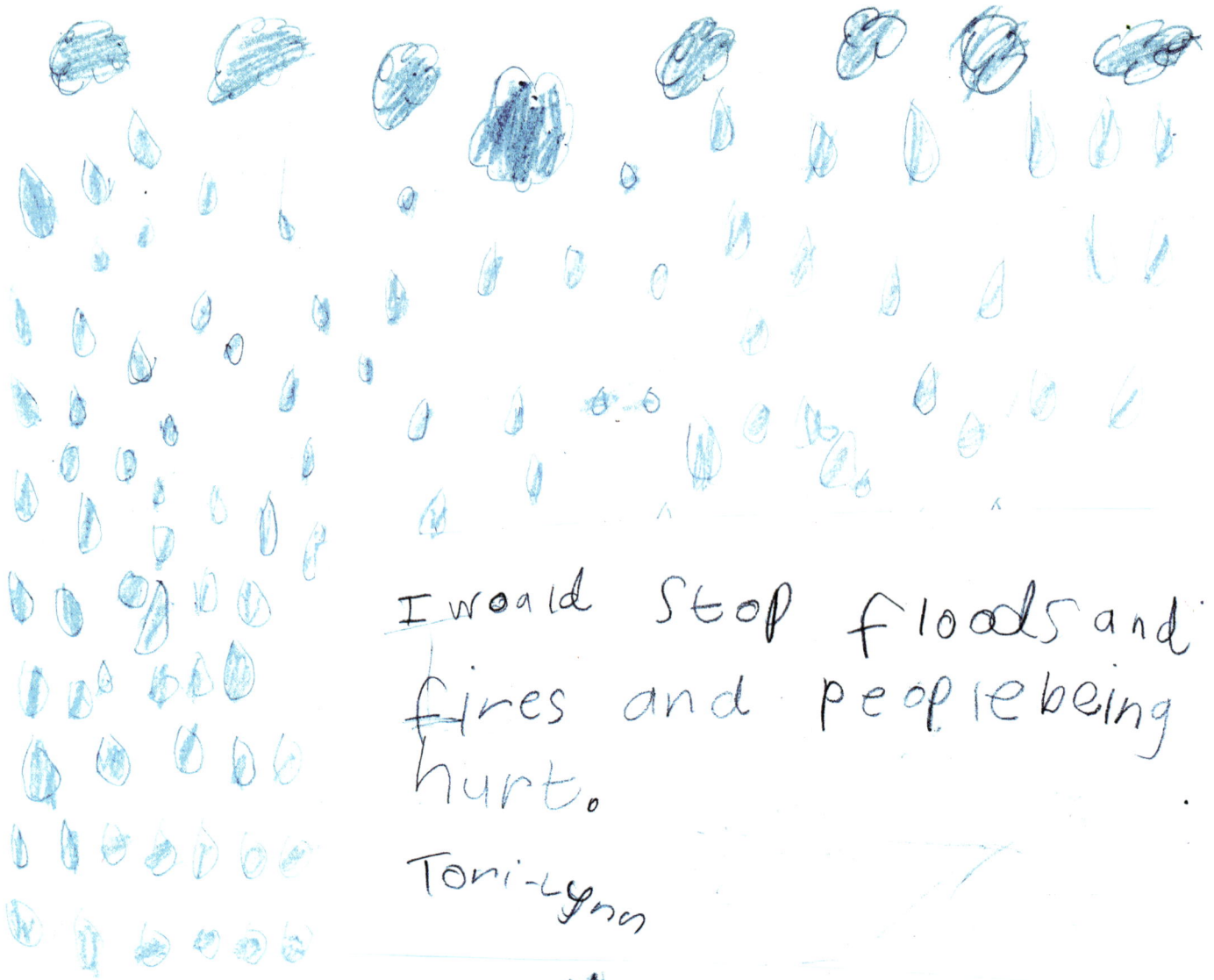

I would stop floods and fires and people being hurt.

Tori-Lynn

Tori-Lynn Kennedy aged 9
Limegrove School Limavady

Rachel Chamberlain
Goodrich CE (VC) Primary School Ross on Wye

Less cars

recycle

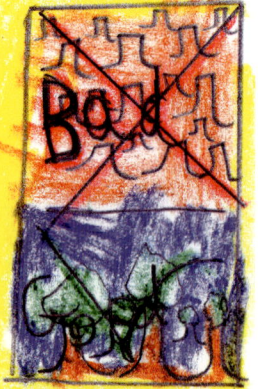

keep trees

Growing more trees

help + tidy up our planet

No Dumping

Dean Cadget aged 11
St Margaret of Scotland Catholic Junior School Luton

182

Adam Shakil aged 11
Hawthorns Junior School Lancashire

If you recycle you will be helping the Environment

Emma Trevor
Coates Lane Primary School Lancashire

184

Not drinking Alcohol

Parks

More

No rubbish on the floor

No Smoking

Angelika Sikorska aged 10
St Margaret of Scotland Catholic Junior School Luton

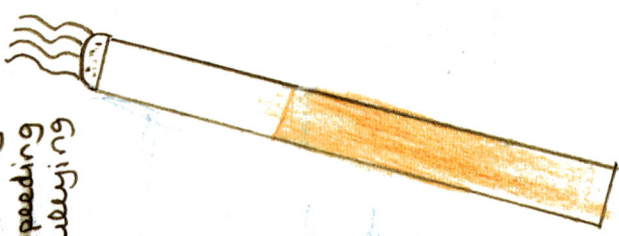

Ali Akbar Hussain aged 10
Hawthorns Junior School Lancashire

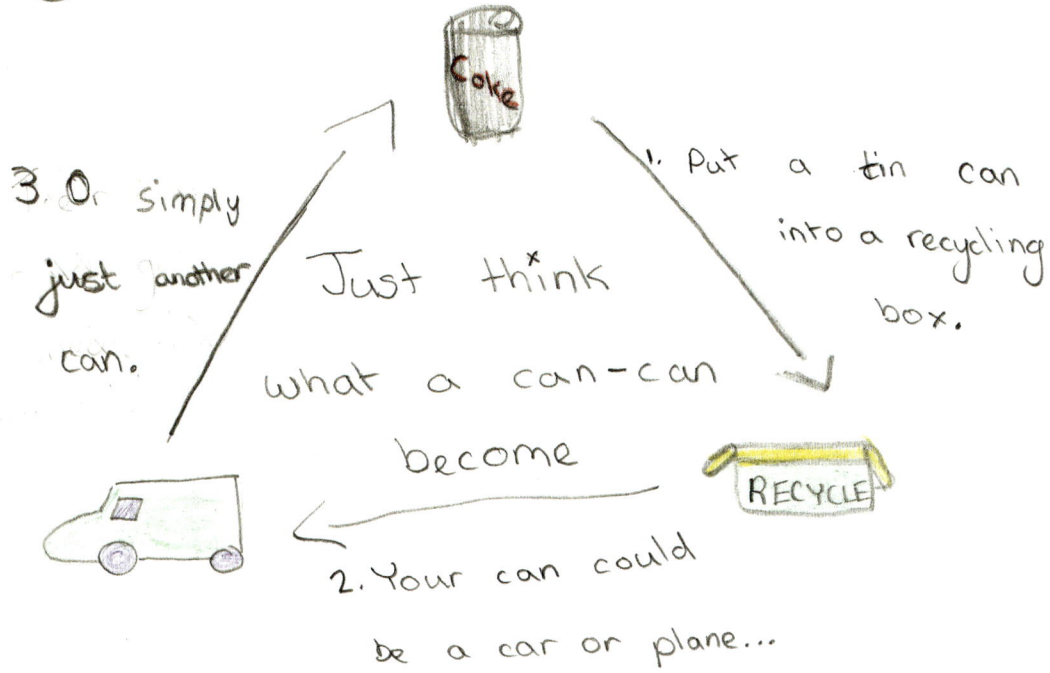

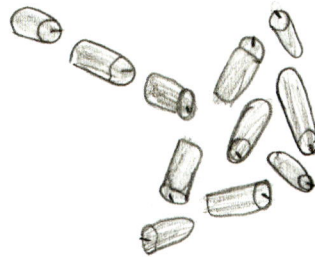

Georgia Ranwell aged 9
Coates Lane Primary School Lancashire

Keep healthy by not taking drugs or not Smoking

Stop all the fightin

And Start doin Some writin.

Look all around you

What do you See

So don't Shut them pins

Put them in the bins

Look what you've done

You've got up and run

You will feel a lot better

So Come on and lets

Make a diffrents

Its your World

Keep the world a happy place

Don't Smoke

I am happy because people have stop fightin

Don't litter

it should be like this

Make A Diffrents

Sarah Jane Lowndes
St Aidan's Catholic Primary School Merseyside

I would stop hurricanes

From knocking peoples houses
down.
I would stop hurricanes

From knocking trees down
and hurting people.

chantelle patton
Fleming fulton school.
Belfast.

Chantelle Patton aged 10
Fleming Fulton School Belfast

Our new world

No gun crime!!!

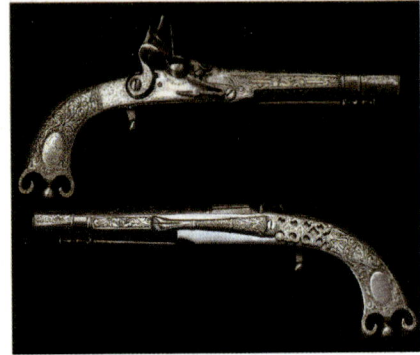

Why kill people!

Poem

People use guns,
When everyone is in bed,
The targets get shot,
And they are dead.

Haiku

Guns are bad to use,
They are to protect people,
Don't use guns to kill!

Sean Paul Hatoum

West Twyford Primary School

London Borough of Ealing   Age 10

This is how I would Improve the world

STOP THE WARS

STOP RAC- ISM

Recycle

If you Recycle paper it would help Stop cutting trees down.

We Should Be friendly with eachother

Don't throw litter on the floor!

Don't WASTE WATER

Sanaa Yr 6
Hawthorns Junior School Lancashire

Improve the world

by Arthur King

Import fair trade goods

Money is fairly spread

Poverty is eliminated

Reduce, reuse, and recycle

Open your minds to pollution

Very rich people must share

Educate every child

Terrorism is wiped out

Happiness for all

Every life is treated well

Welcome all cultures

Obesity is reduced

Regenerate poor housing

Lower carbon footprint

Don't delay start today!

Arthur King
Collis Primary School Middlesex

192

GLOBAL WARMING

Glaciers and ice caps are melting,
Lakes and rivers could dry up
Ozone layer is getting smaller, the Earth is getting
    hotter,
BECAUSE OF US,
Animals are dying,
Listen, how can we help?

We should cycle and share lifts to school,
Ask to have showers not baths,
Recycle, recycle just recycle,
Mum and Dad reuse plastic shopping bags,
If you're not in the room switch off the light,
Never forget that simple things make a difference,
Global warming that's a warning!

"HOW ON EARTH DO WE TURN IT OFF?"

BY:KATHERINE MONKHOUSE, YR5

Katherine Monkhouse Yr 5
St Sebastian's C of E Primary School Berks

Help Make a

CHANGE The country

Things that will happen if we LOOK AFTER your Enviroment:
- The Enviroment will be nice and tidy.
- People will love the view.
- children will be happy where they are playing.

Thing that will happen if we doen't LOOK AFTER your Enviroment.
- The Enviroment will be dirty.
- People will NOT Enjoy the view

Better Place!

Hasnah aged 10
Hawthorns Junior School Lancashire

OUR NEW WORLD

BY AGNES Y.5 WEST TWYFORD PRIMARY

NO GUN CRIME!!!

USE WATER CAREFULLY

RECYCLE

USE WATER CAREFULLY

Give Money To Charities

Agnes Yr 5
West Twyford Primary School London

How to improve the world?

Recycling

1. Don't use things with lots of packaging or wrapping.
2. Re-use things when possible, like using old worksheets as scrap paper.
3. Recycle things like paper, plastic and glass

Set up compost bins
Collect leafs
Dry chippings from chain saw.
grass cuttings
Vegetables
Fruit peels and apple cores.

Don't waste water

Don't leave tap running when watering plants.
Don't fill the bath as full.
Take a faster sure.

Be energy friendly

Turn off lights, computers and other appliances when not in use.
Use compact fluorescent light bulbs to save money and energy.
Insulate your house.
Double glaze windows.

use car less

Instead of using your car walk or cycle.
Share lifts to get to work.

Shania O Boyle
St Brigid's Primary School N Ireland

196

Get Involved

SOLAR ENERGY

GO
GREEN

cut emissions

How to ake the
orld a better ace

WE SHOULD USE
THE MOST ABUNDANT
source of

Jake Kuczogi
St Brigid's Primary School N Ireland

FIGHT FOR FREEDOM!

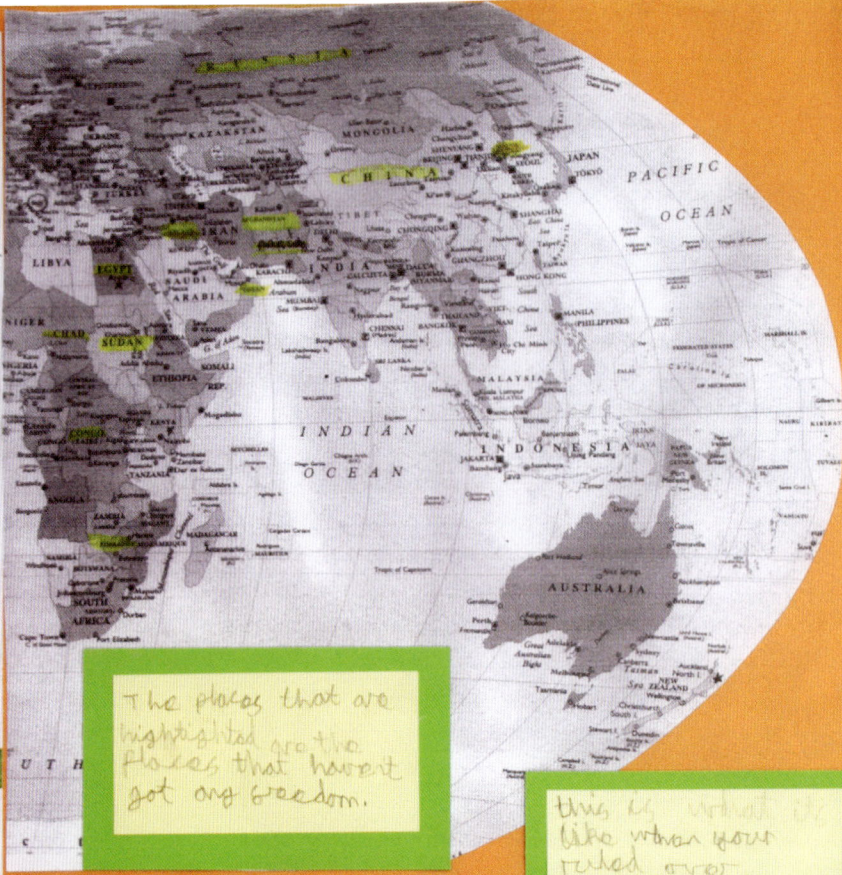

The places that are highlighted are the places that haven't got any freedom.

this is what its like when your ruled over.

Nelson mandela

By Isaac Murphy

he rules over Zimbabwe.

I think that people without freedom should fight for freedom because they should be able to have a choice about their life.

Isaac Murphy aged 9
Newlands Primary School Southampton

Bad side
of
the world

War

If we get too violent
The world will become silent
Stop shooting too much
we will lose our treads
because we none get to try
we don't start
to die.

Smoking

If you smoke
It's not a joke
we'll become unhealthy got.
If we have a fag
we'll become very argh.

Good side
of
the world

recycle

If we all recycle
we can make a new bicycle
Even tho old don't want t
be told
because they don't want to
get cold
So recycle
So recycle

Friend Ship

We love to laugh and play
we do it every day
And we wouldn't want it any other
way.
If we all stay friends
we be able to pass on the trends

By Ben Scandrett, Mathew Morgan and Alex Mills

Ben Scandrett, Alex Mills, Matthew Morgan aged 9 & 10
Budbrooke School Warwick

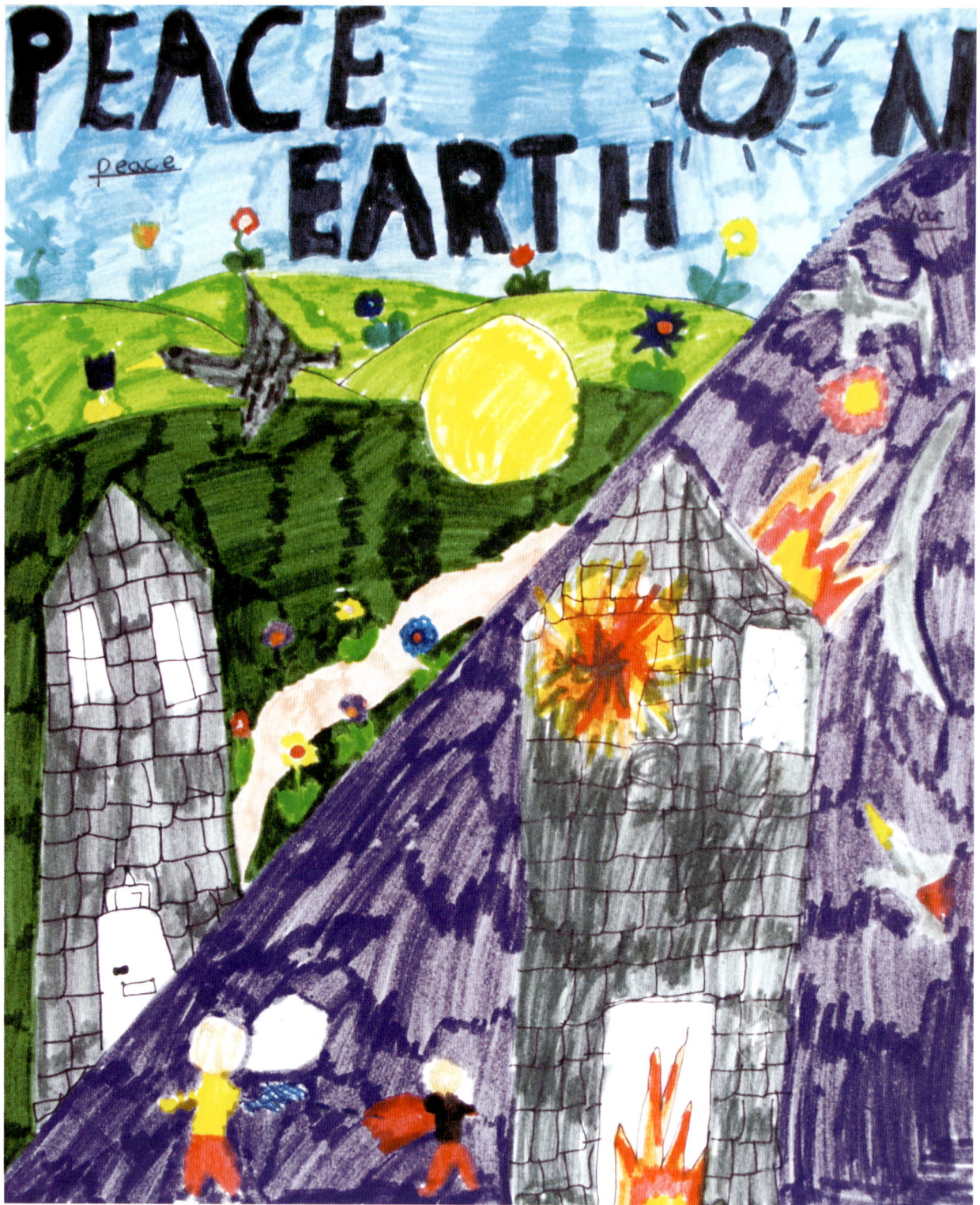

Ryan Miller aged 9
Canmore Primary School Dunfermline

One day there was a lovely village and a hero.

Don't I'm coming

Help Help

I little boy nearbow help because his rubbish was spilt

Demolishing

Disrecycle man

rubbish

always throws

I'm coming

but...

Recycle

end it this going to be the

Ah ah

whoosh away cattle man!

I can again

Liter to People

Joshua Buckingham + Andrew Goode 5/6

Joshua Buckingham, Andrew Goode aged 9 & 10
Budbrooke School Warwick

201

keep our world safe !!!!

KEEP OUR WORLD SAFE

Our Rubbish !!!!

From this

to this

Our world is getting
polluted by chucking
rubbish on the floor,
there are enough bins
to go on around the
world and also we
need to do more recycl-
ing you can recycle:
plastic bottles
cans
paper
glass
tins
you will need to
recycle otherwise our
world will be more
polluted and we would
all die.

X X X X X

FRom this

to this
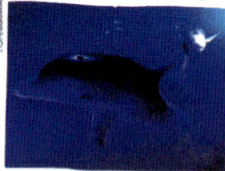

By Jade and
alisha xx

Keep wild Animals Safe!

Every animal deserves to have a life
to live.

Wild animals are getting harmed by rubbish
humans throw. We are throwing their habitat
all away and so they die. Also animals
are getting hurt by glass and other
big land.

Jade Bhatti, Alisha Hatcher aged 9
Newlands Primary School Southampton

Crystal Toppin aged 11
West Twyford Primary School London

This picture of a german sheppard he has been neglected for 2 months.

Poverty is BAD!
Over come it together!
Very true!
Everyone will be happy if you improve!
Renew peoples life!

Together we will improve our WORLD!!!
You and me will do it together!

This bear is made to dance?

Animal Cruelty

This bear is made to dance by people who train him or her. Other animals are being harmed by their owners. Other animals who are being harmed are. whales dogs. tigers. sharks and many more.

P oor P eople

In Africa and countries that are poor, they have nothing. In this picture these two children look like they have no mother or any one who could take care of them. They also have no clothes or shoes. Also they dont have any house

some their country

Anjali Paul aged 9
Newlands Primary School Southampton

204

Improve the world!

Here are a few examples of what our world looks like?

This cat has been locked up.

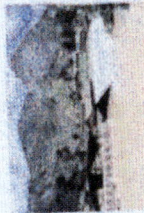

This is a flood in africa.

This dog has been neglected.

LET'S CHANGE OUR WORLD!!!

Thank-you for reading my leaflet!!!

by Anjali Paul!!!

Anjali Paul
Age 9
Newlands Primary School

Anjali Paul aged 9
Newlands Primary School Southampton

205

to make the world A BETTER PLACE!
STOP BULLYING

STOP BULLYING NOW!
TAKE A STAND. LEND A HAND

If you are being bullied, this is what you should do:

1) Walk away. Find some space to think.
2) Tell someone. Whether it be a parent or friend.
3) Sort it out. If you are getting bullied at school, get the teacher to sort it out

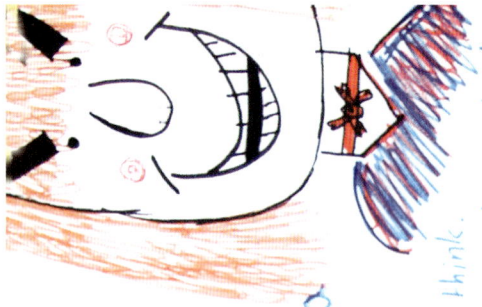

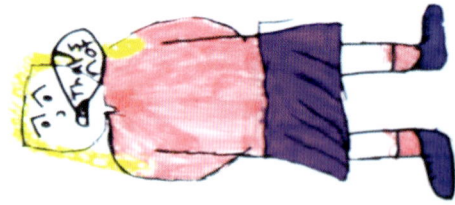

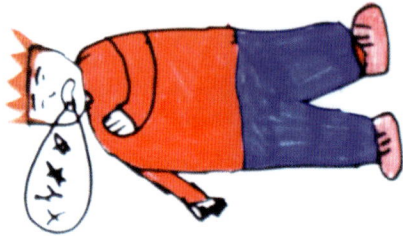

HA HA!

BULLYING is BAD!

Happy for People

Life

HELP SAVE PEOPLE!

BY Effie & Becky & Ralph & Kayah

Effie Seal, Kayah Worrall, Ralph Heaven Richards, Rebecca Swithenbank
Goodrich CE (VC) Primary School Ross on Wye

Cut along the dotted line to make your instruction guide (2 sides)

FOLD

WARNING:
No guarantee can be issued for this product. It is unique.

FOLD

INSTRUCTIONS FOR USE

THE WORLD

James Robertshaw
Collis Primary School Middlesex

Remove product from box and take off any packaging.

1. Start to assemble the major parts; Land, Sea and Atmosphere. You must look after the Atmosphere by removing all greenhouse gasses.

2. Next assemble the houses and factories. As factories are bad for the Atmosphere, you will have to make them Eco-friendly.

3. Start making the shops and farms for food. When growing crops *don't* use to much pesticide or all the plants will be killed off.

4. Ensure that all the countries have a stable government so that they don't wage war on each other!

5. Take care of poor and homeless people that don't have the things we do. Give them a stable income support so they can buy what they need.

6. Try and introduce Fair-trade every where you can so farmers every where get their moneys worth.

FOL

FO

James Robertshaw
Collis Primary School Middlesex

Global Warming Stop!!

Scene 1

(*Enter the room*)
(*Sophie + Natalie throw litter on the floor*)
Chloe: Excuse me I think you dropped something.
(*Sophie point to litter*)
Sophie: What that, I think you find it's called litter.
Chloe: Well put it in the bin then.
Sophie: No way am I going to listen to you.
Natalie: Anyway there are no bins around.
Chloe: You must be blind because there is one right over there.
(*Natalie and Sophie go kick bin over*)
Natalie: Well there is not now!!!
(*Chloe go and pick bin up*)
(*Walk off*)
Chloe: Go ahead carry on if you want your grandkids to die it's fine with me.
Sophie (*Interrupts*): We're not going to have kids.
Natalie: Yeah we're staying single for life.

Scene 2

Chloe: Follow me please. I have something to show you.
Sophie: No way stupid.
Natalie: You will probably kill us or something like that.
Chloe: Don't be silly I'm not that type of person.
Sophie: Fine.
Natalie: Whatever.
(*Follow her*)
Chloe: Well this is it.
Sophie + Natalie: Wow so exciting (*turn around and say not*)
Chloe: That's it I've got you now. I gave you a chance and you blew it. I will now fast forward you into the future.
(*Sophie + Natalie sit in a chair*)
Sophie: Can you remember when we were younger, about the age of 11 when we always wanted to drive cars. Now in the whole 57 years of our life we still haven't driven one.
Natalie: I know and know we haven't got a chance now.
Natalie: I'll call Courtney to make us a cup of tea.
Sophie: No it doesn't matter for me.
Natalie: I'll not have one then.
(*Enter room*)

Scene 3

Courtney: I think I dropped something. How stupid of me.
Sophie: You better pick that up and put it in the bin.
Courtney: Sorry grandma.
Natalie: You better young lady, do you want to kill us.
(*Courtney puts rubbish in the bin and walks off*)

Chloe: Now I will turn you back to normal.
(*Chloe turns Natalie and Sophie back to normal*)
Natalie + Sophie: I am glad we are back to normal again.
Sophie: Do you want a sweet.
Natalie: Please.
(*Natalie and Sophie go to drop their rubbish on the floor then put it in the bin*)

Global warming
Don't do it

Sophie Whiteley, Natalie Bate, Chloe Southall,
Thorne Brooke Primary School, Doncaster

Tyler's Story

How Can We Save the Environment?

We need to save the environment and the animals that live in it and we need to not be cruel to all the animals in the world and give the ones that need our help to save them.

How Can We Help Save the Children?

As well, we need to save the children that need our help and if you were that person how would you feel?...
... How would you stop all the child cruelty?

How can we make the world into a Happy Place to Live?

Wouldn't it be lovely to see all Children Smiling?
How can we make that happen?

Here are my suggestions:

1   No more cruelty

2   Teach everyone to be kind to others

3   Help those who cannot help themselves

4   Help to raise money for different charities

5   And help the ones that need food and a warm bed

Tyler,
St Sebastian's Primary School, Berks

Make tomorrow better!!!

SONG:

C'mon lets change the world,
C'mon lets make the world a better place
(x2)

Stop the poaching, it's bad for the animals,
Stop the poaching, it's sad and cruel

C'mon lets change the world,
C'mon lets make the world a better place
(x2)

Money isn't equal, compromise I'll be fair,
Money isn't equal let the people have a share

C'mon lets change the world,
C'mon lets make the world a better place
(x2)

Stop bad pollution, it's destroying the place,
Stop bad pollution, it's bad for the human race

C'mon lets change the world,
C'mon lets make the world a better place
(x2)

C'mon lets change the world
NOW!!

Bethany Parsons, aged 11,
Newlands Primary School, Southampton

The world in which we live

Has many resources to give
But they will soon run out
If you do not listen to my shout
Reduce, reuse, recycle quick
Together we can make good habits stick

We must tread with care
So as not to pollute the air
We must only use a car
When we want to travel far
Trains and buses are the best
Because they're greener than the rest

Many animals are becoming extinct
Because people don't stop to think
Save the animals is what I say
Don't do it tomorrow do it today
Stop destroying their habitats
Because you know you wouldn't like that!

If people would only please
Stop cutting down all the trees
Preserve the forests save the trees
And help to make the planet breathe
It would really help to save the Earth
We have to decide how much it's worth

Martha McKenna, aged 10,
The Grange Junior School, Cheshire

Peaceful World I Wish!!

SONG:

Come on man take a ride with me,
From Portadown to Newry,
Everything is cool as can be in a,
Peaceful world I wish.

People know this world is troubled,
I'm sick and tired of killing and robbing,
The criminals made it worse and worse,
Watching what working class people are doing.

These are just words and words are ok,
It's what you do and what you say,
So don't despair.

Come on man take a ride with me,
From Portadown to Newry,
Everything is cool as can be in a,
Peaceful world I wish.

If I could stop this killing and robbing,
And let our children out to play,
Without the fear of trouble coming our way,

Hatred to each other is not ok,
I'm not the ruler of the world,
I'm just a little schoolgirl,
Who would like to make the world a better place,
So don't despair.

Come on man take a ride with me,
From Portadown to Newry,
Everything is cool as can be in a,
Peaceful world I wish.

Listen to me as you travel with me,
From Portadown to Newry,
Everything is cool as can be in a,
Peaceful world I wish.

The money's good and the works ok,
So I don't see why it's not ok,
Be careful with your heart and what you love,
Make sure it is sent from above,
It's what you do and what you say so don't
despair.

Come on man take a ride with me,
From Portadown to Newry,
Everything is cool as can be in a,
Peaceful world I wish.

Listen to me as you travel with me,
From Portadown to Newry,
Everything is cool as can be in a,
Peaceful world I wish.

Hey yeah!
Hey yeah!
Oh yeah!

Kathryn Abraham,
Hart Memorial Primary School, N Ireland

I believe we could save our planet by doing lots of things. Here are some of my ideas:

We should save energy which we can start doing at home by switching off lights and all other electrical appliances when not in use. This can also be done at school, at work etc...Other ways that we could save energy would be to use energy efficient bulbs, small windmills for electricity, solar panels on roofs to power our homes.

We have problems with waste and recycling. There are many things we could do to improve this:
We should recycle all materials that should be recycled by making sure we put the correct things into the proper bins and banks. We should also try not to waste water because so many people use water when it is unnecessary.

And then we have pollution! We can't miss it because it is everywhere. There are so many different ways in which we are polluting our planet. We should be walking and cycling to school if possible.

Using vehicles pollutes the air which we are all breathing. We should be using bio diesel.

Littering is a huge problem because most of it is not bio degradable, not only is it untidy and smells but it can cause pollution in rivers where people dump their waste. So put your litter in the bin!

Industrial pollution pollutes the atmosphere because factories send out smoke. Factories must find other ways or fuels which don't pollute the atmosphere.

Pollution is killing us, animals, the earth and the atmosphere!!! We should love and respect our beautiful world and the wonderful things it's given us. We should also care for our planet and all the living things that are on it.

IT'S NOT JUST HUMANS THAT NEED LOVE!

Ronan Karicos, St Brigid's Primary School, N. Ireland

Animal Rap

Tigers are dying
People are lying
They think they're making money
But they're not even funny.

Dolphins getting extinct
You better think!
What you doing? What you doing?

Danna na na don't shoot it.
Danna na na don't shoot it.

Hunting hunting isn't good
It making the animals in a mood
Don't see the point for hunting food
You're up to no good.

Da na na na na na na na don't shoot it
Da na na na na na na na don't shoot it
Da na na na na na na na don't shoot it

Reiran Parker, Anthony Purcell, Bud MaCauley, aged 10,
Newlands Primary School, Southampton

Better World

Song

Making people happy and laugh out loud
Showing everyone you're a smiling cloud!

Why destroy when you can find and make?
Let's re-cycle, let's re-create!

We should come together and do our chores.
We've got all we want so why make wars?

Get more water for Africa,
Help them survive all disaster.

That's what'll make a better world,
That's what'll make a better world,
So come on let's make a better world,
Come on let's make a better world,
Oh come on yeh!

Let's stop destruction – in a world of strife,
Let's give people a better life.

Let's stop the war happening in Iraq
Let 'em go home let the soldiers pack

No more violence! Let the animals be!
No more hunger or poverty.

No more guns. Stop global warming,
This is our message – the peoples warning!

That's what'll make a better world,
That's what'll make a better world,
So come on let's make a better world,
Come on let's make a better world,
Oh come on yeh!

Smoking and drugs will harm your veins,
Destroy your body and bring you pain.

Come on let's give some charity
To help the poor get aid help the blind to see

Let's help the poor get food and money
And help the children who have no mummys

Let's rescue the children living on the streets
Let's give them some shelter and food to eat

That's what'll make a better world,
So come on let's make a better world,
Come on let's make a better world,
Oh come on yeh!

(repeat)

The world is dying
The children are crying
Donate your money
So they can keep healthy

(repeat x 4)

**Harriet Duke, George Halligan,
Rhys Fitzsimons, Andrew Vare** (aged 10)
**Kate Howard, Lindsay Radford,
Lizzie Stansfield, Tom Partridge,
Yasmin Ali, Charley Booth**
(aged 11)
Dowson Primary School, Cheshire

With local songwriter – **Andy Perry**

Index

Elizabeth Greenwell	St Margaret of Scotland Catholic Junior School	Luton	44
Elizabeth Massey	Highclare School	Birmingham	161
Elizabeth Rogers	Goodrich CE (VC) Primary School	Ross on Wye	148
Ella Hutton	Longwick C of E Combined School	Bucks	22
Ellie and Hannah	St George's School for Girls	Edinburgh	16
Ellie Huxtable	Budbrooke School	Warwick	151
Ellie Lancaster	Goodrich CE (VC) Primary School	Ross on Wye	152
Ellie Molloy	St Aidan's Catholic Primary School	Merseyside	160
Ellie Roper	Goodrich CE (VC) Primary School	Ross on Wye	152
Ellis McGlynn	St Aidan's Catholic Primary School	Merseyside	106
Emily Boulton	Castle Primary School	Somerset	31
Emily Carter	St Cecilia's Catholic Primary School	Surrey	144
Emily Jones	The Grange Junior School	Cheshire	161
Emma Barnsley	Budbrooke School	Warwick	151
Emma Jones	Moorfield Primary School	Cheshire	163
Emma O Hagan	St Aidan's Catholic Primary School	Merseyside	47
Emma Robertson	Canmore Primary School	Dunfermline	58
Emma Trevor	Coates Lane Primary School	Lancashire	184
Flora Blake-Parsons	Collis Primary School	Middlesex	139
Fran Furniss	Longwick C of E Combined School	Bucks	40
Frank Hills	Thorne Brooke Primary School	Doncaster	50
George Brooker	Longwick C of E Combined School	Bucks	21
George Halligan	Dowson Primary School	Cheshire	214
Georgia Davies	Braunston C.E. School	Daventry	179
Georgia Leggott	Thorne Brooke Primary School	Doncaster	70
Georgia Leggott	Thorne Brooke Primary School	Doncaster	71
Georgia Needham	Longwick C of E Combined School	Bucks	22
Georgia Ranwell	Coates Lane Primary School	Lancashire	187
Gillian Crisp	St John's Primary School	Barrhead	112
Giovanna Scozzari	St Cecilia's Catholic Primary School	Surrey	120
Grace Cain	Budbrooke School	Warwick	126
Grant Ogilvie	Canmore Primary School	Dunfermline	150
Guy Molony	Collis Primary School	Middlesex	75
Hannah Cargill	Lavant House	Chichester	128
Hannah Chandler	St Cecilia's Catholic Primary School	Surrey	45
Hannah Clarke	Budbrooke School	Warwick	126
Hannah Gunn	St George's School for Girls	Edinburgh	67
Hannah Mogford	Clun Primary	Neath	110
Hannah Moriarty	St Cecilia's Catholic Primary School	Surrey	136
Hannah Scothern	Coates Lane Primary School	Lancashire	91
Hannah Webber	Newlands Primary School	Southampton	167
Harrie Wheatley	Thorne Brooke Primary School	Doncaster	24
Harriet Duke	Dowson Primary School	Cheshire	214
Harvey Brook	Rodborough Community Primary School	Stroud	9
Hasnah	Hawthorns Junior School	Lancashire	194
Hattie Lewington	Braunston C.E. School	Daventry	95
Haveesa Kaneez	Hawthorns Junior School	Lancashire	99
Helen Nzubi	St Margaret of Scotland Catholic Junior School	Luton	155
Henry O'Niell	Deerhurst and Apperley Church of England School	Gloucester	167

Holly Pettifor	St Sebastian's C of E Primary School	Berks	162
Hope Warner	Highclare School	Birmingham	107
Hugh Thomas	Budbrooke School	Warwick	171
Isaac Murphy	Newlands Primary School	Southampton	198
Jack Beinck	Budbrooke School	Warwick	159
Jack Cullimore	Rodborough Community Primary School	Stroud	105
Jack Grey	Longwick C of E Combined School	Bucks	32
Jack Knox Mackie	Thornwood Primary School	Glasgow	133
Jack Sinclair	Thornwood Primary School	Glasgow	53
Jack Walmsley	St Sebastian's C of E Primary School	Berks	72
Jack Whittaker	Goodrich CE (VC) Primary School	Ross on Wye	13, 20
Jade Bhatti	Newlands Primary School	Southampton	202
Jade Davies	Clun Primary School	Neath	61
Jade May	Newlands Primary School	Southampton	140
Jake Appleton	Longwick C of E Combined School	Bucks	89
Jake Church	Rodborough Community Primary School	Stroud	63
Jake Kuczogi	St Brigid's Primary School	N Ireland	197
Jake Taylor	Thorne Brooke Primary School	Doncaster	50
James Robertshaw	Collis Primary School	Middlesex	207, 208
James Savage	St Aidan's Catholic Primary School	Merseyside	29
Jamie Donnelly	Budbrooke School	Warwick	88
Jane	Coates Lane Primary School	Lancashire	38
Janet Kelly	St Brigid's Primary School	N Ireland	147
Jasmine Gosney	Castle Primary School	Somerset	131
Jasmine Webb	Braunston C.E. School	Daventry	46
Jed Palmer	Rodborough Community Primary School	Stroud	101
Jenna Massey	Thornwood Primary School	Glasgow	9
Jenny Ansell	Braunston C.E. Primary School	Daventry	52
Joe Ferguson	Rodborough Community Primary School	Stroud	58
Joe Woodward	Budbrooke School	Warwick	88
Joel John Armstrong	Hart Memorial Primary School	N Ireland	104
Jordan Swindells	Moorfield Primary School	Cheshire	10
Jordan Young	Thorne Brooke Primary School	Doncaster	58
Joseph Owen	Budbrooke School	Warwick	159
Joshua Brown	St Sebastian's C of E Primary School	Berks	156
Joshua Buckingham	Budbrooke School	Warwick	201
Joshua Cromie	Fleming Fulton School	Belfast	80
Jude Dillon	St Brigid's Primary School	N Ireland	158
Kate Howard	Dowson Primary School	Cheshire	214
Katherine Monkhouse	St Sebastian's C of E Primary School	Berks	193
Kathryn Abraham	Hart Memorial Primary School	N Ireland	212
Katie Ashforth-Shaw	Rodborough Community Primary School	Stroud	64
Katie Sheath	Newlands Primary School	Southampton	167
Katy Frith	The Grange Junior School	Cheshire	17
Kayah Worrall	Goodrich CE (VC) Primary School	Ross on Wye	206
Kayne Forshaw	St Aidan's Catholic Primary School	Merseyside	154
Kerry Friel	St John's Primary School	Barrhead	162
Kieran Lowley	Goodrich CE (VC) Primary School	Ross on Wye	86
Krystian Maksymiak	St Margaret of Scotland Catholic Junior School	Luton	114
Laura Pennell	Longwick C of E Combined School	Bucks	40
Laura Taylor	Moorfield Primary School	Cheshire	102
Lauren Durrant	Longwick C of E Combined School	Bucks	36

Lauren Hand	Thorne Brooke Primary School	Doncaster	56
Lauren Martin	St Brigid's Primary School	N Ireland	127
Lauren Millen	Thorne Brooke Primary School	Doncaster	58
Leona McManus	Limegrove School	Limavady	25
Liam McCann	Moorfield Primary School	Cheshire	140
Liam Smith	Moorfield Primary School	Cheshire	144
Liam Toland	Limegrove School	Limavady	96
Liana Rosewell	Longwick C of E Combined School	Bucks	36
Libby Swan	Lavant House	Chichester	121
Lindsay Radford	Dowson Primary School	Cheshire	214
Lizzie Stansfield	Dowson Primary School	Cheshire	214
Lucy Whitehead	Budbrooke School	Warwick	151
MacKenzie Wells	Newlands Primary School	Southampton	169
Maddi O'Niell	Deerhurst and Apperley Church of England School	Gloucester	167
Marc Miller	Canmore Primary School	Dunfermline	33
Margrete Urquhart	St George's School for Girls	Edinburgh	122
Marguerite Parker	St George's School for Girls	Edinburgh	168
Martha McKenna	The Grange Junior School	Cheshire	211
Martin Curren	St John's Primary School	Barrhead	163
Martin Falls	Limegrove School	Limavady	30
Matthew Campbell	Canmore Primary School	Dunfermline	54
Matthew Crawford	Hart Memorial Primary School	N Ireland	172
Matthew McMullan	St Brigid's Primary School	N Ireland	153
Matthew Morgan	Budbrooke School	Warwick	199
Megan Coates	Fleming Fulton School	Belfast	165
Megan McLaughlin	Limegrove School	Limavady	170
Megan McLean	St John's Primary School	Barrhead	138
Megan O'Toole	St Aidan's Catholic Primary School	Merseyside	146
Megan Singleton	Castle Primary School	Somerset	132
Megan Webb	Longwick C of E Combined School	Bucks	177
Megan Welsh	Thorne Brooke Primary School	Doncaster	58
Megan Wickins	Lavant House School	Chichester	64
Megan Young	Thornwood Primary School	Glasgow	102
Meghna Rao	Lavant House School	Chichester	14
Melissa Smith	Thorne Brooke Primary School	Doncaster	58
Mellisa Mastertin	St George's School for Girls	Edinburgh	67
Michelle McMullan	St Brigid's Primary School	N Ireland	105
Mike Toole	Longwick C of E Combined School	Bucks	32
Millie White	Goodrich CE (VC) Primary School	Ross on Wye	152
Monica Molina	Lavant House	Chichester	145
Morgan Jenkins	Clun Primary School	Neath	130
Morgan Murphy	Thorne Brooke Primary School	Doncaster	58
Nadia Stewart	Thornwood Primary School	Glasgow	61
Naomi Boobbyer	St Sebastian's C of E Primary School	Berks	166
Naomi Cribson	Deerhurst and Apperley Church of England School	Gloucester	167
Natalie Bate	Thorne Brooke Primary School	Doncaster	209
Natasha Duffy	St George's School for Girls	Edinburgh	69
Nathan Johnston	Fleming Fulton School	Belfast	15
Niamh Quinn	Fleming Fulton School	Belfast	125
Nicholas Topping	Hart Memorial Primary School	N Ireland	169

Nicola Kennedy	St Margaret of Scotland Catholic Junior School	Luton	23
Nicole Cathcart	St John's Primary School	Barrhead	163
Nicole Myers	Thorne Brooke Primary School	Doncaster	58
Nuala-Beth McKeown	Budbrooke School	Warwick	83
Oliver McCaffery	The Grange Junior School	Cheshire	100
Olivia Exan-Treckett	The Grange Junior School	Cheshire	19
Olivia Frances	Braunston C.E. Primary School	Daventry	131
Olivia Hinkley	Rodborough Community Primary School	Stroud	129
Olivia Leach	Collis Primary School	Middlesex	172
Olivia Tenquist	The Grange Junior School	Cheshire	110
Padraig Magee	Fleming Fulton School	Belfast	48
Padraig Marshall	Fleming Fulton School	Belfast	34
Paris Johnson	Lavant House	Chichester	124
Patrick McCrystal	St Brigid's Primary School	N Ireland	63
Peter Taylor	Goodrich CE (VC) Primary School	Ross on Wye	86
Peyton Sims	Longwick C of E Combined School	Bucks	22
Philippa Bricklebank	Braunston C.E. School	Daventry	10
Phoebe Snow	Goodrich CE (VC) Primary School	Ross on Wye	152
Rachael Rice	Fleming Fulton School	Belfast	55
Rachel Chamberlain	Goodrich CE (VC) Primary School	Ross on Wye	148, 181
Rachel Hartin	Limegrove School	Limavady	35
Rachel Kelly	Hart Memorial Primary School	N Ireland	64
Rachel Pond Thorne	Brooke Primary School	Doncaster	56
Rachel Thomas	Clun Primary School	Neath	131
Ralph Heaven Richards	Goodrich CE (VC) Primary School	Ross on Wye	206
Raoul Hodgson	Rodborough Community Primary School	Stroud	136
Rebecca High	St John's Primary School	Barrhead	14
Rebecca Hupp	St George's School for Girls	Edinburgh	50
Rebecca Swithenbank	Goodrich CE (VC) Primary School	Ross on Wye	206
Rebecca Whitelaw	Limegrove School	Limavady	43
Reece Crawford	Canmore Primary School	Dunfermline	52
Reece Rigby	Moorfield Primary School	Cheshire	54
Regan McIlveen	Hart Memorial Primary School	N Ireland	176
Reiran Parker	Newlands Primary School	Southampton	213
Rhianna Mills	Budbrooke School	Warwick	83
Rhianne Baxter	Rodborough Community Primary School	Stroud	142
Rhiannon Phelps	Lavant House	Chichester	77
Rhys Fitzsimons	Dowson Primary School	Cheshire	214
Rhys Owen	Goodrich CE (VC) Primary School	Ross on Wye	13, 20
Rianna Jackson	Fleming Fulton School	Belfast	76
Richard Lewis	Clun Primary School	Neath	14
Rob MacKinnon	Thornwood Primary School	Glasgow	134
Robert Fayolle	Budbrooke School	Warwick	59
Robin Graham	Hart Memorial Primary School	N Ireland	167
Ronan Karicos	St Brigid's Primary School	N Ireland	65, 213
Rosie Haynes	Braunston C.E. School	Daventry	39
Ryan Miller	Canmore Primary School	Dunfermline	200
Ryan Smith	Thornwood Primary School	Glasgow	50
Ryhima Jadoon	Hawthorns Junior School	Lancashire	100
Saif Bashir	Hawthorns Junior School	Lancashire	118
Sam Owen	Clun Primary School	Neath	53

The footprints we make-

The children will take.

What legacy will you leave?

What future do you weave?

For your children...

and your children's children.

Walk in Beauty